Always

Always

written and compiled by
SUZANNE NEWMAN
featuring several collaborations with
MICHAEL GRGICH

RESOURCE *Publications* · Eugene, Oregon

ALWAYS

Resource Publications
An Imprint of Wipf and Stock Publishers
199 W. 8th Ave., Suite 3
Eugene, OR 97401

www.wipfandstock.com

PAPERBACK ISBN: 979-8-3852-2753-2
HARDCOVER ISBN: 979-8-3852-2754-9
EBOOK ISBN: 979-8-3852-2755-6

VERSION NUMBER 07/19/24

CONTENTS

Section Two

Section Three

Section Four

PREFACE

So, why is this book called "Always?"

The title came to me because it struck me that God is always there for us, and we can always approach Him in prayer 24/7. We can always be honest with Him in a way that is unique and not possible with any other person, and He always knows what we want and need. The Lord always deals with us in grace and love, and He is always faithful.

We are always developing our relationship with The Lord throughout our lives, and there is always something new to be found in The Bible that we haven't leant before. . .there is never a time where we think we know everything. We are also always discovering things about ourselves as human beings and as individuals and can always reflect on how good God is to us in all circumstances in His mercy and never-ending grace.

There will always be difficulties in life to face, and there are always struggles to fight our way through (whether that be grief, mental illness, physical health concerns etc.). We will always have our faith in God tested in some way and we are always under spiritual attack from The Devil, our human sinful nature and this fallen world's temptations. That having been said, believers are always able to withstand whatever life throws our way because we are always safe in God's care. He always gives us blessings and support in any dark, difficult times. We always wear His armor. We can always rely on Him to fight for us, and we know He will always forgive us our sins when we are truly sorry and repentant. We are blessed that our transgressions are covered by The Lord Jesus Christ, always and forever, by His blood and victory at Calvary.

Praise to The Father,
Praise to The Son,
Praise to The Holy Spirit. . .
ALWAYS.

INTRODUCTION.

Hi! My name is Suzanne Newman and I live in England. I became a born-again Christian at the age of 19yrs. The Lord put the gift of poetry on my heart after my cancer journey in 2015/16 and I have been avidly writing it ever since! I only write poems with a reassuring Christian message, even when the topic is about depression, anxiety, grief etc. I do write pure praise pieces sometimes, but mostly my poems are about the struggles we all face in life, based on my own personal experiences. I often put some sort of twist in my writes to make them more fun to read, for example, I will compare anxiety to a runaway train, or self-doubt as an imp on my shoulder whispering in my ear etc. I have tried to cover a mixture of topics in this book.

I share my poems on Facebook with the hope of somehow encouraging others in their faith who struggle in similar ways to me. In this sense, I have had a lot of positive feedback so far. All glory goes to God, who never leaves us to battle alone during difficult times and holds us securely in His unfailing love and grace. I am amazed at the various gifts God gives all of us in different ways and I am grateful and humbled to be merely His servant in this small way right now, acknowledging I am nothing and can write nothing without Him.

I met Michael Grgich via Facebook soon after I joined, and we have been writing Christian collaborations together since 2020. He writes poems on similar subjects to me, so we gel well together on the message we convey to readers, which is all to God's glory. We also run a Christian group together called "Faith, Hope and Love" and have brought out two Christian poetry books together, called "Inspired By. . ." and "Kindred Spirits".

SECTION ONE

All poems written by Suzanne Newman.

"SO YOU DON'T HAVE TO."

I bled so you don't have to,
Drank God's cup of wrath instead of you,
I took your place upon the cross,
I paid the price, so you're not lost.
I suffered much, so you don't have to,
Went through hell instead of you,
I gave my life, so you don't die,
And you get to share my Heaven's skies.
I battled sin so you don't have to,
Broke all chains, in love, for you,
I came to Earth to take your place,
And show you God's unfailing grace.

"A JOURNEY OF BROKEN SHARDS."

The broken shards of my broken life
Lay scattered across the bathroom floor,
Where the broken shards of my broken peace
Make these pilgrim's feet bleed, 'til they pour,
The broken shards of my broken dreams
Have fallen in the corner's cracks,
And the broken shards of broken joy
Are covered in dust and tears of black.

I try to collect these broken shards,
That have scattered so high and scattered so far,
But as I attempt to pick them up,
My fingers, thumbs, and palms get cut.
These shards are sharp like razor-blades,
And slice so deeply from life's pain,
I look around, and simply cannot see
How these shards are of any use to me.

I fall down on the floor in pieces,
Amongst the blood and broken pieces,
Don't know why life fell to pieces,
But I pray to God to help me fix these pieces.

The Lord views me with compassionate eyes,
Because He is gracious, loving, and kind,
And then my wounds He tends and binds,
And gifts me peace and hope inside.
God takes these broken shards of mine,

Holds them in His potter's hands Divine,
And reassures me when He deems it's time,
He will help me make a masterpiece so fine.

Restoration and creation,
I see is possible from this devastation,
Soul and faith say I must simply trust
The one who grants me sweet Salvation.

And, gradually, every broken bit
Starts to slot in place and somehow fit,
No longer injuring me with nicks,
But building a picture, through God's mosaic.

By using faithful eyes to see,
I can make vague sense of what's before me,
Not everything, but enough to see,
How The Lord is shaping and maturing me.

This restoration is still incomplete,
I'm still broken in places, head's messy not neat,
But I walk life's mosaic with pleased pilgrim's feet,
Trusting God every day, 'til my journey's complete.

"I'M READY, LORD."

You have come for me, Lord. . .I sense you near me,
I see angel wings and doves quite clearly,
I feel the icy fingers of death,
Creep around my throat to steal my breath.

I'm ready, Lord,
And have been every day of my mortal, fragile life,
Since the day that I was blessed and saved
By the power of The King. . .Lord Jesus Christ.
I fear not the valley, its shadows, nor death,
For faith is sure and your promises I'll not forget,
I'm ready to ascend your Heavenly steps,
The Devil can't have me. . .much to his regret.

So, take me Lord,
I am not scared,
I don't know what to expect,
But I know you're there,
I trust you in death,
Just as I have in life,
And I give my soul gladly
To The Truth—Jesus Christ.

I'm ready, Lord,
And as I groan my final, struggled human sighs,
I feel warm angels' wings surround,
And gently close my mortal eyes.
I hear your peace-doves cooing, Lord,

Like a serenade that sings me soft to sleep,
And sends me on my eternal journey,
Where I'll rest with you in everlasting peace.

"SILENCED."

"Keep quiet," says depression's chilling voice,
Choking vocal cords so I have no choice,
One hand is firmly across my mouth,
To ensure I cannot scream or shout.

Taken hostage by this icy black,
Which ties my tongue up from the back,
So I'm forced to say that I am fine,
Whilst brain's left pickling in this brine.

Can't ask for help, because this brute,
Keeps a firm grasp, so I must stay mute,
He's a kidnapper lurking under my skin,
A parasite taking me over within.

I feel him crawling around inside,
I scratch and rub, but still he hides,
Elusive presence—everywhere yet nowhere,
Unobservant eyes can't see he's there.

Depressions hands are clammy and cold,
Their withering touch makes me feel old,
I hate the smell of his dark, long fingers,
And the taste of helplessness he makes linger.

Smothering words and rising the tides,
He whispers damning critique and lies,
Hissing and slithering through my brain,
And oozing out into my eyes and veins.

Soon I feel his hands all over me,
Leaving tidal marks and dark debris,
I can't see straight, and can hardly breathe,
As rationale bobs in his murky seas.

But, in this storm within I find,
My faith stays strong and isn't blind,
And soul can see a lighthouse tall,
Shining out a beacon from our loving Lord.

God's my anchor, so I won't drift far,
He's my life-ring within this sticky tar,
Depression can never really smother me,
For God hears my heart and silent pleas.

And depression's hands grow weak before
The awesome power of our mighty Lord,
So, even when silenced, I need not fear,
For the narrow way stays well-lit and clear.

"THE REAPER AND THE SON."

The Grim Reaper's used to harvesting spirits,
But not so with Jesus—he couldn't go near His,
For up on the cross it was already given,
When Christ's work was finished, to The Father in Heaven.

So, The Reaper wasn't quite sure just what to do next,
And paced up and down by the cross, most perplexed,
The scythe by his side was swinging redundantly,
As he pondered the figure, hanging there at Calvary.

The Reaper's confused, irritated and stressed,
But still satisfied with The Christ's lifeless flesh,
He smiles when he smells death and sees people mourn
The loss of this Jesus, whom they do call "Lord."

The Reaper observes as they pierce The Christ's side,
And all do agree on His Earthly demise,
The body's un-nailed and lowered down from the cross,
Carried carefully by kin, who wrapped Him up in a cloth.

The Reaper then follows them to the grave room,
Watches on, quite intrigued, as Christ's sealed in the tomb,
Double-checks life's bereft and a dead body lays
In the form of this Jesus—God's Lamb who was slain.

The Reaper hasn't got Christ's soul at his command,
And just hovers around, rubbing cold, empty hands,
He's used to collecting the spirits he reaps,
To deliver them to either Hell or Heaven to keep.

The Reaper does loiter for a great length of time,
Just itching to check on this body, Divine,
But sees he's no power to interfere with
The Holy process, that The Lord knows is His.

Then, The Reaper is suddenly blinded by light,
When the huge tombstone's moved, by Heaven's great might,
This figure of death is brought down to his knees
In awe, watching Christ—risen Lord—walking free!

The Reaper is stunned by The Savior of Man,
Who holds life and death in the palm of His hand,
The Reaper bows, dumbstruck, awestruck, and agog,
At the power of this invincible, uncontrollable, God.

Sin, death, grave and Hell are not Jesus's keepers,
He shines as The Victor, smiling at The Grim Reaper,
Who stays on the ground, as his blackened heart pounds,
Watches Christ walk away, without making a sound.

"HAND IN HAND."

The Devil lurks and prowls around,
Waiting to devour me on cold ground,
He offers up his devious hand,
To try and steer me in the desert lands.

He says that he can support and help,
But I hear his drooling hellhounds yelp,
They howl in hunger and feed on fear,
But soul's warning bells ring loud and clear.

I know The Devil is natural liar,
Who never quashes but stokes trial's fire,
So I will never take his hand,
But shall put my trust in God's great plan.

This pilgrim may be torn and beat,
But I'll never cede, or admit defeat,
I'll hobble on my weary feet,
And keep walking down the narrow street.

God's with me, so heart and soul leap
With joy and hope and love so sweet,
For I'm a saved and much blessed sheep,
And God comforts me as I strain and weep.

The Lord's the only help I seek,
And He gives me strength when I feel weak,
My faith's sure, 'though the outlook's bleak,
So I'll dis Satan's lures and lies so sleek.

So, hand in hand across difficult land,
I'll walk with God, who'll help me stand,
And soon The Devil slinks away,
With his hellhounds and their haunting bay.

In any wilderness, God will see me through,
And the walk by faith has a glorious view.

"IT'S NOT MAKE-UP. . .IT'S WARPAINT."

I don't wear make-up, I put warpaint on,
So other people cannot see
The eyebags, worry-lines and flaws,
That show up the battles inside of me.

I don't wear make-up, I put warpaint on,
So other people won't suspect
The stress and strain within my brain,
That leaves my peace of mind just wrecked.

I don't wear make-up, I put warpaint on,
So other people think I'm fine,
They don't want to see this haggard mess,
And I don't want to face their question time.

I don't wear make-up, I put warpaint on,
Not just outside, but inside as well,
For every day's a battlefield,
Against the spiritual foes of Hell.

I battle against my weaknesses,
I battle against The Devil's lies,
I battle against the trials of life,
And the mental ills that claw my mind,
I battle against my sinful nature,
I battle against my physical pain,
I battle against life's pressures,
And the weight of responsibilities great strain.
I battle with sword gripped in my hand,

I battle with helmet firmly on,
I battle with shield held strongly up,
And I'll battle hard the whole day long,
I battle against my huge self-doubt,
I battle against the dark I see,
I battle as a Christian soldier of faith,
For I know The Good Lord fights for me.

"WHEN."

Will you miss me when I leave one day?
When The Reaper comes to take me away,
When he swings his scythe to slice and slay
My body, in death's dark mists of grey.

Will you miss me when there's nothing left?
When my bones are swallowed up by death,
When I've no more words nor mortal breath,
And soul's ascending Heaven's white steps.

Will you miss me when I'm in a box. . .
A wooden coffin with flowers upon the top,
Remember, it's just my flesh that rots,
For soul's saved by The Risen Christ and cross.

Will you miss me and the love I gave?
Any pearls of wisdom, please do save!
Please know I don't remain death's cold slave,
As my soul gets raised from this Earthly grave.

I'll be happily dwelling in Heaven's peace,
All my worldly angst and pain will cease,
And I'll gladly bow at Lord Jesus's feet,
And thank Him for calling me into His keep.

So, don't miss me, for I'll not really be gone. . .
I'll simply change residence and just move on,
To join all the saints and great Heavenly throng,
And sing The Lord's praises all day and night long.

"SHADOW-MAN."

There is a creeping shadow-man,
Who follows me around,
He hides inside my silhouette,
That stretches upwards from the ground,
And everywhere I turn, he's there,
Some days he looms so large,
He makes me shaky and nervous,
Through my thoughts he seems to run and barge.

This shadow-man is traumas past,
That won't seem to release me,
Which haunt like specters in the night,
And tinge the light of day I see.
Depression's also shadow-man,
Whose icy presence lingers,
Just itching to consume my mind,
With blackened, sticky fingers.

This shadow-man is paranoia,
No confidence and plump self-doubt,
Which tells me that I'm rubbish,
And no-one cares if life would take me out.
Some days this shadow-man is quiet,
His presence low-key, outline small,
But other times, he's looming large,
Shouts loud, looks like a huge brick wall.

Most days he comes to run me down,
Fills my ears up with woes and taunts,

Reminds me of my battle-scars,
And bad relationships that haunt.
I try to beat-down shadow-man,
And sometimes I succeed,
Pep-talk myself it's not all bad,
And try to boost my self-esteem.

But someone also walks with me,
That keeps this shadow-man at bay,
Christ Jesus stands beside me,
Son of God, to chase the dark away.
Christ tells me that He supersedes,
All troubled thoughts and nagging doubt,
That He has dealt with my past,
And that HE can chase all demons out.

So, shadow-man is swallowed-up
By Christ's own power and awesome figure,
When shadow-man comes looming large,
He finds Christ Jesus stands much bigger!
And what great solace, then, to know
That I don't walk alone,
For my constant friend, companion,
Stands with me from His great Heaven's throne.

"A SEASONED SAILOR."

Lord, I'm not a seasoned sailor,
I don't have the skills to stay afloat,
In this dark tempest brewing,
Where life's troubled seas do rock my boat.
I'm frightened, Lord, and blundering. . .
Why don't you calm this looming storm?
My weak and praying hands shake,
My poor rudder's snapped, and sail is torn.

Dear child, just trust me in this trial,
Rest in your faith. . .it's strong enough,
Know I won't leave you all alone,
Shan't let you drown when seas get rough,
Whilst I COULD calm this storm, I won't,
For it will teach you vital skills,
Then, in time, you'll discover
You ARE a seasoned sailor, and fears are stilled.

It takes no skill or effort
To sail calm waters' gentle, lapping waves,
Nor faith or perseverance,
When all is tranquil on a sunny day,
You grow much stronger, learn new things,
When you've fought through great tempests,
Please trust I shall equip you,
And know your soul's at peace, and rests.

"OUT-SINGING THE CROWS."

In God's strength, I'll out-sing the crows
That squawk at me with mocking tones,
Who perch upon the cold, harsh graves,
Which trials of life have carved and made.

For sorrows try to bury me,
While ravens hop around in glee,
And pointy-beaked and jet-black rooks
Twinkle beady-eyes with evil looks.

The vultures long to peck my flesh,
As I lay, a weeping, weary mess,
The cemetery of my woes,
Cries "doom" in icy winds that blow.

The tombstones grin with sickly smiles,
Invite me in, to dwell a while,
The yawning holes dug in the dirt,
Wait to consume, in pain and hurt.

But I'll not give up willingly,
Still raise my praise-voice joyfully,
Remind the grave and mocking birds,
That God's with me and God has heard.

He's heard my tears and sees my plight,
And in the dark, He remains the light,
No satanic calls, or evil screech,
Can push me past Lord Jesu's reach.

For He's The Victor of the grave,
The King and Lamb, who bled and saves,
And in Him I'm not scared of Hell,
And won't succumb to sorrow's yell.

So, I will out-sing every crow,
And won't be plucked by clawing toes,
And do not fear the grave's dark hole,
For God's the keeper of my saved soul.

"I SERVE A LIVING GOD."

I don't serve a long-dead, absent Lord,
Whose life ran out when His blood poured,
Upon the cross on Calvary's hill,
'til His mortal flesh hung cold and still.
For this is not the end, you see,
When Christ conquered sin for you and me,
In order for death to set us free,
He needed to rise up in victory.

And, on day three, this is what He did,
When He left the tomb all evil hid,
For now, The Lamb's a lion as well,
Triumphant over sin, the grave, and Hell.
And Heaven sounds the great trumpet call,
To hail the Almighty King of all,
Who dwells in Glory on His throne,
Interceding for us, until we're called home.

In the meantime, the good Lord helps us through,
All stresses and strains life drags us through,
Christ shares His righteousness with us,
Cleanses and perfects us by His blood.
He walks beside us every day,
Talks to and guides us on our way,
I feel Lord Jesus lives in me,
And in all His children that I see.

Yes. . .Jesus is alive and well,
Calling people daily away from Hell.

He died on the cross, don't be mistaken,
His human form was dead and taken,
To a new and unused burial tomb,
Wrapped and sealed up in this dark, stone room.
But afterwards, God's power and grace,
Did work great miracles in this place,
'til Jesus, on that blessed third day,
Was resurrected, alive, and not the same,
As that battered man up on Calvary,
For now nothing and no-one stands above He,
Who IS The Savior, Lord, and Messiah,
Who cares for us all and gifts Spiritual fire,
Until that day when He'll come again,
To harvest the Earth and the souls of all Men,
And, THEN the whole world will bow its knees,
To the living God that I love, serve, and see.

"THE REAPER FLOATS ON DEPRESSION'S TIDES."

The Reaper paddles through depression's tides,
Which engulf and then settle in my mind,
He runs his scythe and bony claws
Along the dank, cold, oppressive walls.

The Reaper lurks in the misty gloom,
Enjoying the smell of impending doom.

He bides his time and gayly floats,
In an ominous, jet-black, eerie boat,
Whose fearful creaks and damp, dark groans,
Strike terror into my shaking bones.

The Reaper knows depression well,
And has seen many souls fall to its swell.

The Reaper thinks that it won't be long
'til I cease singing hope's sea-shanty song,
He knows his boat can take the weight
Of two bodies, so he sits and waits.

The Reaper sees how depression floods,
How it addles the brain and infects the blood.

The Reaper admires depression's walls,
The confusing maze that its bricks do forge,
He sees how my head is dull and sore,
As he stirs up the silt of its ravaged floor.

The Reaper's task is to take our lives,
Thus, transporting our souls to the afterlife.

The Reaper feels at home in the dark,
Doesn't like the light's optimistic spark,
He roots for depression's black to win,
So he can paddle over to drag my lost corpse in.

The Reaper watches pitch waters run,
And waits for suicidal thoughts to come.

But, The Reaper is in for a huge surprise,
For my soul has been saved by Jesus Christ,
And, as such, He is my buoy and guide,
And firm anchor within depression's tides.

The Reaper knows God's light too well,
And knows He rescues His sheep from Hell.

The Reaper concedes that God will win,
Depression won't drown me, for I shall swim,
And God will keep my head above
These deadly waters, in His grace and love.

So, The Reaper turns his boat around,
When he sees I'm standing on Holy ground.

The Reaper bows in reverence to Christ,
Who says He'll summon him when it's time
To take my life, heart, flesh, and bone,
And He'll send an angel to guide soul home.

The Reaper understands and smiles,
Knowing that my struggle will be worthwhile.

The Reaper knows kin of The Lord Most High,
Don't surrender in battle, won't cede, and die,
For God provides light, strength, and hope,
And manna and stamina, so then we can cope.

The Reaper steers his boat and leaves,
Nods to me as a faithful one who believes.

I thank God for His love and support,
For His guiding hands and His sheltering port,
I'll grow stronger and wiser with God by my side,
And will find a way through depression's dark tides.

"BEFORE THE LORD."

I was broken and sick,
With a hard, swinging brick,
In the space where my soft heart should be,
With a gaping great hole,
Eating up my poor soul,
Where this world and its sin consume me.

I was troubled and lost,
With the weight of sin's cost,
Just a nomad in search of a home,
Didn't buy Satan's lies,
Nor this realm's veiled disguise,
I felt empty, bereft, and alone.

It was dark—no joy spark,
Shadows in every part,
As I searched for the answer and cure,
But no respite or light
Were found anywhere in sight,
So, I walked 'til pilgrim's feet became sore.

Then, on one cloudy night,
To my relief and delight,
I heard The Good Shepherd call out my name,
In a flash of pure light,
All was happy and bright,
As my soul was freed of sin and shame.

Jesus filled up my hole,
Gave me peace in my soul,
In the space where my emptiness was,
And Redemption's pure spark
Chased out all trace of dark,
Hallelujah! I'm saved. . .thank you God!

Then Salvation, Divine,
Did at last become mine,
Due to Christ's victory, love, and grace,
With the blood He infused,
My heart's full and renewed,
And my soul can now touch Heaven's gates.

"HARDSHIP."

Hardship is a brutal man,
With big, bruised knuckles on both hands,
His voice booms and can't be ignored,
As he shouts and pounds on my front door.

He smirks and tips his big top-hat,
His teeth, just like his hat, are black,
He smells of rotting flesh and flames,
And his job is to inflict great pains.

Hardship is friends with The Devil,
Who, we all know, likes to rile and meddle,
They hope, together, to cause such heat,
I'll lose faith and be dragged underneath.

Hardship kicks with hob-nail boots,
'til there's blood and dirt stains on his suit,
He smokes cigars so long and thick,
And the smell and smoke make me feel sick.

Hardship studies his pocket-watch,
To check if he's been on time or not,
He's prompt, as usual, to his satisfaction,
And he longs to see my scared reaction.

Although he's daunting, I won't lie,
I'm defiant, and stare him in the eye,
I shan't be beaten, cede, or die,
For I'm bold in Christ, who's by my side.

Hardship's surprised and disappointed,
For his dark plan's foiled and all disjointed,
But still, he manages to inflict pain,
Hoping that I'll never rise again.

Although I lay in a crumpled heap,
I smile at him through blood-stained teeth,
My black eye hurts and bruised cheek pounds,
But I pray whilst kneeling on the ground.

I pray for wisdom, courage, and strength,
For God to straighten this path that's bent,
That He'll fight for me, for I am done,
But my faith's still strong in The Risen Son.

Hardship mocks, but soon is shocked,
By a blinding light which leaves him rocked,
For Jesus comes to say "enough!"
And tells Hardship not to play so rough.

The Lord gives me a helping hand,
Lifts and supports, so I can stand,
In time, He sends Hardship away,
And reveals His purpose for this pain.

I'm sure I'll meet Hardship again,
Whether material, physical, or in my brain,
But with every battle I'll claim victory,
All thanks to God for never failing me.

"NEED."

Do I need to speak a little louder, for you to hear me, Lord?
Do I need to pray more often, 'til my voice croaks and my throat is sore?
Do I need to talk persistently, go to church, or raise my hands, or kneel?
Do I need to shout to reach the heavens? For I must express, Lord, how I feel.
Do I need to use big, fancy words for you to understand my needs?
Do I need to quote you Scripture, or just show you where my sorrow bleeds?
Do I need to put my pain in verse, or write a lamentation's song?
Do I need to fast, sleep, then repeat? Please show me where I'm going wrong!
For I've not received an answer to my eager prayers in quite some time,
And I fear within my current trial, your guiding light has lost its shine.

There's nothing "wrong" my troubled child,
Be patient and wait for the time,
That I choose to respond to you,
In mysterious ways, and grace, Divine.
Be reassured, I hear your prayers,
No need to make a scene and shout,
I listen to your heartfelt moans,
When verbal words have long run out.
So, lose your desperation, child,
Have faith and leave things in my hands,
Remembering you are not alone,
Just trust my ways and Holy plan.

"THE DARK VERSUS THE LIGHT."

Some days I fear the dark may win,
For its hands are strong and its grip is grim,
The dark The Devil throws my way,
Entices sin to come and play,
Whilst this world's a challenge, every day.

Some days I fear the dark may win,
For it fogs my head and creeps under skin,
The dark will goad and poke and shout,
My mental ills all swirl about,
Thoughts flood and rage and won't drain out.

Some days I fear the dark may win,
For it recalls all my faults and sin,
The dark does prod low self-esteem,
Pops hope's bubbles and destroys sweet dreams,
It churns up stress and troubled seas.

Some days I feel the light will win,
For I've been freed from past and all sin,
And I'm held safe in Jesus Christ,
Who comforts me on long, dark nights,
And fills my heart with His love's light.

Some days I feel the light will win,
When I greet the morn with a grateful grin,
For I trust The Lord with my life and time,
Have faith in His grand plan, Divine,
And I'm joyous I'm His and He is mine.

Some days I feel the light will win,
For the Book of Life has MY name in!
So, I have nothing left to fear,
I fight on, knowing God is near,
And when I need Him, He's always here.

Some days I feel the light will win,
And douse the fiery furnace I'm in,
For I'm not left to burn and die—
I'm protected by The Lord Most High,
So, my blessed soul can sing and fly.

Every day I know the light will win,
For I'm God's, and nothing's greater than Him,
And any darkness I may go through,
Still won't obstruct sweet Heaven's view,
So, joy's tears shine like morning dew.

"POUNDING ANXIETY."

Anxiety's a monster truck,
A bronco that goes wild and bucks,
It races round your mind untamed,
Whilst screeching like a runaway train.

Anxiety's a yapping dog,
It squeals shrill, like a frightened hog,
Bounds through your thoughts like a leaping gazelle,
Whirl-winding peace into merry Hell.

Anxiety's a thunderstorm,
Whose rumbles make the scared mind worn,
It pitter-patters like cold hail,
Makes faces long and drawn and pale.

Anxiety's like Dracula,
Draining life from the mind's main jugular,
Haunts like some big, grey, hovering specter,
A vampire bee that sucks your nectar.

Anxiety's a racing horse,
That runs but can't complete the course,
A music box with broken tune,
Whoops cruelly, like a fierce baboon.

Anxiety chips at the mind,
It wears like two millstones that grind,
It rushes through your brain and thoughts,
Like tidal waves in which you're caught.

Anxiety's a pounding nag,
A marathon that makes you flag,
Serenity falls through your fingers,
Rearing panic lasts and lingers.

Anxiety's a broken treadmill,
Mind is racing, gallops uphill,
Screams at you just like a child,
And whirlpools round, with rapids, wild.

Anxiety is stomach-churning,
Frantic cogs which spark whilst turning,
"What-if's" scurry through the brain
Like a thousand mice, to drive you insane.

Anxiety creates such trouble,
Mashes all ration into a puddle,
A technicolor blur of stress,
Like toddlers' paintings—just a mess.

Anxiety's a carousel,
With warped music that's sent from Hell,
The horse's hooves pound on the ride,
That never stops, just dizzies, blinds.

But, when you close your eyes and breathe,
Pray to The Lord for some relief,
And focus on that Holy bond,
Anxiety cannot stay for long.

For God is comfort, strength, and rest,
And helps worn minds to know they're blessed,
Retrains the brain towards His will,
And calms the storm. Says: "Peace. Be still."

"JUST CALL ME HUMAN."

You will say that I'm not a "real Christian,"
You will claim I don't use 'proper' words,
You will say that I'm simply a hypocrite,
You will think that I must never curse.
You will say that my mind shouldn't struggle,
You spout that some things I do aren't 'right,'
You will say that I must be your doormat,
And my behavior's not much like The Christ.

Don't call me names. . .
Just call me human!

Yes, I must try a lot harder,
And, yes, I do need to improve,
Yes, sometimes I lose my temper,
And, yes, I get in a bad mood.
But this doesn't mean I'm not Christian,
It means I'm flawed and doing my best,
I try every day to do better,
But I'm human and feel pain and stress.
Being Christian means I trust in Jesus,
I've been saved by His power, love, and grace,
I acknowledge I remain far from perfect . . .
That only happens when I'm through Heaven's gates.
So don't ever question my loyalty,
Nor my love and dedication to God,
I'm devoted to serving Him the best that I can,
But I'm still human. . .why do you think that's odd?

So, please don't you call me names, my friend,
Don't push your idealism onto me,
Don't jibe at me with your warped prejudice,
And don't lecture on what I "ought" to be.
I know I'm just a huge work in progress,
I don't need you to point out where I lack,
Give yourself a dose of your bad medicine,
And don't hurl knives deep into my back.

I won't let you goad, bait, or belittle me,
Won't allow you to make me doubt myself,
I pray to The Lord for assistance,
Guidance, and wisdom, when I need His help.
I trust in all of Jesus's promises,
I'm saved in His love, victory, and grace,
Unlike you, He won't tut and then criticize,
When life's trials make tears run down my face.

Christians still feel strain and pain, friend,
If you prick us, our flesh will still bleed,
We're not all immune to stress and hurt,
We fall short of imitating Christ's lead.

So, climb down off that great tall pedestal,
You know, this one you built for yourself,
Don't speak to me so sanctimoniously,
From your judging, ignorant, lofty shelf.
I AM Christian, I'm just not flawless,
'though I stand guilt-free in Jesus Christ,
So, before you throw stones this way, my friend,
Look at your own glass house and maybe think twice!

You're not perfect, so open-up your eyes,
Look past the mirror, and peer deep inside,
You're in no position to criticize,
Others who God does accept, love, and prize.

Don't call me names. . .
Just call me human!

"GOD'S KINTSUGI POTS SHINE."

(Kintsugi is the Japanese art of putting broken pottery pieces back together with gold—a metaphor for embracing your flaws and imperfections and creating something even more beautiful than before).

I'm just a chipped, fragmented, faded pot,
Quite worn with many deep, dark cracks,
Others see the surface flaws I show,
But only God knows my warped, broken back.

It's hard trying to keep it together,
When I have much weight to carry each day,
My remnants are weakened and rattle,
And there're war-wounds and scars in my clay.

I worry sometimes I'll just fall apart,
Get swept up by life's uncaring broom,
These days, mornings all seem much darker,
Heart hangs heavy and is full of such gloom.

I'm trying to un-frown my sad face,
Where I don't feel like smiling a lot,
I often feel like a poor, useless burden,
Just a broken and worthless old pot.

But The Lord made me this way on purpose,
Not because He's uncaring or cruel,
But, because I still work 'though I'm fractured,
And all flaws are, in fact, useful tools!

The Lord holds me together each difficult day,
And ensures I won't crumble apart,
He reminds that my soul can't be broken,
And puts comfort and hope in my heart.

The Lord helps me carry life's burdens,
And encourages me to speak up,
And to tell of His goodness and purpose,
To fellow cracked and strained pots and cups.

The Lord gives us loads we must handle,
But doesn't give more than we can each bear,
He will carry us when we are struggling,
Tends and loves us in His awesome care.

The Lord's our Creator and Sustainer,
Master potter, and we're all His clay,
Whilst some vessels seem pristine and perfect,
Each is damaged in some hidden way.

Our faith in The Lord just grows deeper,
With each crack and chip that does appear,
We rely on His grace and compassion,
Knowing He hears us and always draws near.

We can use our cracks to assist others,
Show how resilient God makes us despite,
And there's beauty and reasons for our flaws,
Which shine brightly when The Lord does highlight.

So, we mustn't hide away or be downcast,
Nor ashamed of our weakened, dark cracks,
For God fixes them up with His pure gold,
And ensures we're alright and don't lack.

With each part He mends that shimmers with gold,
So much more of The Lord will be shown,
And less of these poor human vessels,
Then, God's power can be seen, heard, and known.

"WARPAINT."

I'm a crumbling, dark, depressive clown,
Who no-one really sees deep-down,
Below the bright and thick make-up,
Drawn on like a mask when I wake-up.

I cover up blemishes and all cracks,
Conceal my pain, and mental black,
No-one can mock what they can't see,
So, I won't expose the inner me.

Eyeliner's applied like dark warpaint,
Pink lipstick frames a smile that's fake,
Below this strained, frustrated grin,
I'm exhausted. . .dying. . .deep within.

But I make others happy, coz that's what I do,
Despite of any pain that I'm going through,
I only let God see the real me inside,
For He's the safe place which I run to and hide.

So, the world shall not see the tired tears that I cry,
For I ensure that cosmetics are amply applied,
And humor and smiles are good guises for show,
For they camouflage well, the sad clown who I know.

The warpaint and mask are protection for me,
To cover up vulnerabilities I want no-one to see,
But, with God I am honest, for He comforts and loves,
And strengthens in a way that only comes from above.

And God accepts me, flaws and all, as I am,
Doesn't judge or over-burden me, unlike fellow Man,
When I'm exposed and bare-faced with my Father and King,
I'm blessed with sweet relief and the peace this does bring.

"PALACE."

I'm standing, agog, in the palace I've built,
The bricks are my shame, my wrongdoings and guilt,
Each block is a sin, filled with selfish, vain pride,
The mortar's regret, which cements me inside.

I can't budge these walls, as they're now in the past,
The present can't touch them—their history lasts,
Hindsight—that cruel mistress—laughs that it's too late,
Can't erase what I've done and now sealed is my fate.

On the outside this palace looks fine to the world,
Shiny structure of fun, with huge towers that curl,
But my soul looks inside, without base human eyes,
And sees it's a prison, with no spiritual prize.

I smell the rank air, for sin's putrid and rotten,
The tears my soul cries make the ground wet and sodden,
The murky, damp air gives a menacing laugh,
Which echoes around every stairwell and shaft.

I see Satan tapping his fingers with glee,
As he lurks in the dark, biding time 'til he grabs me,
I don't know when and how that I got so trapped,
But it must have been when self-control went and snapped.

And, now, I stand here watching time ticking by,
With no view of God's glory, for this structure's too high,
'though I crick my poor neck, all I see is more wall
Reaching up to the sky, and I'm left feeling small.

With each day that passes, my sin adds more bricks
To this palace of shame, that leads to Satan's pit.
The good deeds I do, can't remove all the bad,
And, disheartened, I dwell. . .feeling hopeless and sad.

But here in the depths of my guilt and despair,
A soft knock on the door reverberates through the air,
I rush through the palace, my heart racing fast,
Blocking out all the screams of my transgression's past.

I ignore self-doubt and The Devil's sweet-talking,
Pay no heed to this world and society's balking,
I run to the front door as fast as I can,
To be greeted by Jesus—Savior, God, Son of Man.

We have a big chat. I confess as I pray,
And I hear every word that The Christ has to say,
He offers to destroy my great palace of sin,
Gift rebirth to my soul, who pleads "yes", with a grin!

Willingly and gratefully, I let Jesus through,
He enters inside and surveys the grim view,
He looks at me kindly—grace and love outpour,
He accepts my apology. . .lets me call Him Lord.

"Don't worry", He says, "I forgive you, my child",
As I fall to my knees, with a huge, relieved smile,
And, as I am filled by The Spirit's great fire,
Holy flames burn my palace, on sin's funeral pyre.

With one wave of His hand, Christ removes all my guilt,
There's no sign of the prison that my filthy hands built,
"Now, let's start afresh!" Jesus says in His love,
As I stare reverently, at the great view above.

"STILL."

I still dance upon sore, tired feet,
Still kneel in awe when knees do bleed,
I still smile 'though my eyes may weep,
For The Lord is always good to me.

I still fight when I'm worn and beat,
Still hold shield up and won't retreat,
I still stand and let my Jesus lead,
For The Lord is always good to me.

I still praise when mental ills do feed,
Still won't hunger. . .for I've all I need,
I still witness and shan't ever cede,
For The Lord is always good to me.

For my soul's calm. . .at peace. . .and still,
Rests easy. . .sleeps. . .and fears no ill,
Knowing Christ has paid off my sin's bill,
And 'though I'm flawed, God loves me still.

This world may leech and drink its fill,
Satan tries to bend me to his will,
Temptations call with voice so shrill,
But God shepherds, and He loves me still.

"GALLEONS AND DRIFTWOOD."

I'm clinging onto driftwood, Lord,
Whilst bobbing in these troubled seas,
I'm frightened, stressed and flagging,
And feel jellyfish around my knees.

I'm tempted to let go, my Lord,
And sink into the silent depths,
I'm confused and frustrated,
And now struggle just to gasp a breath.

My weary legs can't kick, Lord—
Haven't strength to swim and glide along,
My heart is weighing heavy.
These determined arms. . . no longer strong.

I see the light ahead 'though, Lord,
And know that's where I need to be,
I'm not sure I can make it. . .
That horizon's so far off for me.

There're others heading that way, Lord,
Who sail upon fine galleons!
Skim easily across the waves,
Magnificent, like racing stallions!

Their ships put me to shame, Lord,
Leave me tossed within their joyous wake,
I pray that you'll provide some
Understanding, in your wise name's sake.

Then, Jesus walks across the waves,
To join me where I eddy round,
Encourages me to hold on
To His grace and this new faith I've found.

He points out many others
Who, like me, are clinging onto planks,
I see they struggle also,
But still persevere and give Him thanks.

Christ says if I look closer
At the galleons, they're not all they seem,
Most are just fake cardboard facades,
Whose sailors ride denial's dreams.

And flimsy ships will fall apart
When stormy oceans surge along,
They float in clement weather,
But then quickly sink when things go wrong.

But there are still some galleons
Who ARE strong and true and built to last,
Made up of lots of driftwood planks,
Which they collect from trials past.

The sailors are a faithful few,
Who let God steer their craft ahead,
Towards the light of Heaven,
On the edge of earth, where angels tread.

And maybe one day, in the future,
I'll build me a galleon, true,
When I have learned the lessons
I require to have a better view.

But Jesus reassures me that
It matters not HOW I'll arrive,
On galleon or driftwood,
So long as I use faith to ride rough tides.

For Heaven takes all-comers,
Not just those who bound on in with glee!
The gates are also open to
The ones who crawl on broken knees.

Bedraggled from the trials of life,
Sore finger-tips from clinging on,
Believers ALL are welcomed,
By the Lord who keeps souls safe and strong.

So, thank you Lord. . .I'll persevere,
Through testing times and harsh, cruel seas,
I'll hold on to my faith, and trust
The Savior who does rescue me.

"WHEN IT'S RAINING INDOORS."

On the outside, I may seem just fine,
But I'm slowly drowning on the worn inside,
For tears that won't show on my face,
Build up inside, at tsunami's pace.

This salty brine wears out the heart,
Seeps into every emotional part,
Erodes the body. . .unbalances mind,
Where negativity's cruel and unkind.

Egged-on by self-doubt, guilt and stress,
These waters churn, leave joy a mess,
They fill my legs and middle too,
Then chest and arms, 'til I'm soaked through.

Up to my neck in tears within,
Each waking moment's long and grim,
My inner peace swims for its life,
And eddies round in current strife.

I feel as 'though I cannot breathe,
Where this crying offers no relief,
It doesn't seem to ease the pain,
Still frustration bubbles and doesn't drain.

But, deep inside me, untouched by my wailing,
Is my redeemed soul, staying dry, whilst she's bailing,
Her feet are not wet, for she stands on The Rock,
Which rises above heartache, grief, pain and shock.

Soul lives in a house that The Lord God has built,
Lives happy and safe, free from past life and guilt,
She looks to the future, where there is no pain,
No crying in Heaven, where bliss falls like rain.

Soul calls to my mind and heart with a great shout,
Stands tall, unafraid, unashamed, wings spread out,
She roars at the tears and the water that builds,
Telling it to recede, for this core spot is filled!

Emboldened in Christ, Soul has staked out her ground,
Which is Holy and sacred, where true peace is found,
The waves rush and froth, but have powerless foam,
And they cannot reach up to soak Soul's happy home.

Soul then slowly walks in her sanctum of peace,
Gently closes the door and thanks God on her knees,
She quietly, reverently, speaks to The Lord,
And explains all my pain, and why my tears pour.

Soul knows that The Father, The Spirit and Son,
Will gift hope and reassurance, while these waters run,
God gives me compassion, love, cares in great grace,
And refocus the mind onto trusting in faith.

And God will soak up all my tears like a sponge,
Refill heart with such peace, tell all fears, "move along,"
Christ Jesus will share all my burdens and pain,
Whilst The Spirit's great fire evaporates all the rain.

I feel so much better now the cruel tide is broken,
And thankful to God, rested, now we have spoken,
I felt all alone, but know that's not the case,
For the great Triune God's omnipresent, in grace.

So, thank you dear Lord, I know when tears run,
That you won't let me drown, your love and power bung
The two holes, (known as eyes), from which pained waters flow,
And you fill them with hope, and a blessed, peaceful glow.

"WRESTLING WITH SELF."

My opponent's quite formidable,
And wants to hold on to my soul,
Won't release it easily to God,
And tempts me with a knowing nod.

She tells my soul we'll have more fun
If we DON'T go with God The Son,
For we'll enjoy more guilt-free things
If we don't admit that they are sin!

This foe that's trying to twist my arm
Is "old-self," who deceives with charm,
She has a nervous, masking smile,
Lives in a dark house called "Denial".

She doesn't want to kneel and pray,
Is selfish, refusing to obey,
She wants to win, and grabs my throat,
And wrestles "new-self" on the ropes.

My soul's alarmed "old-self's" so near,
Hears the poison she drips in my ear,
Feels vicious kicks and fists rain down,
As she tries to knock Redemption's crown.

But soul's assured we're saved by God,
And this crown can never be dislodged,
Salvation cannot be reversed—
Deflects all schemes, however perverse.

And just as "old-self" thinks she's winning,
She spots "new-self" is calm and grinning,
Realizes that old love's replaced,
By the love for Christ and saving grace.

Heartbroken, beaten, but won't go quiet,
"old-self" stomps round, creates a riot,
Says that she'll fight me everyday,
But my soul ignores her and turns to pray.

"old-self's" attacks can be quite cruel,
But "new-self's" strong, and ain't no fool,
And redeemed soul can always take the knocks,
For its feet stand firm, on God's own rock.

I wrestle in life's ring each day,
'gainst "old-self" who rears up to play,
But since I'm reborn and renewed,
I'll fix my eyes on Glory's view.

And I know I'll win every bout,
For "old-self" carries no real clout,
Her challenges won't better me,
Can't hold my soul, for it's safe and free.

"EVERY."

Every brutal nail that pierced His skin,
Was one in the lid of the coffin of sin.
Each strike of iron through The Christ's great hands,
Brought sin closer to being under Holy command.

Every drop of The Lamb's blood that spilled
Upon the cross, at Calvary's hill,
Created a step on the Holy stairs
That lead up to Heaven, so WE can dwell there.

Every pain-filled tear that Jesus shed,
Took Him closer to the brink of death,
But still He fought in love and grace,
To win Mankind Salvation's place.

Every mocking voice that cried aloud,
Added to the weight of His thorny crown,
Each scratch and tear and pointy prick
Resembles each of Satan's tricks.

Every piece of Scripture that's fulfilled,
Ensured Christ did The Father's will,
And took Him so much closer to
Making sure that sin was run right through.

Every aching bone and oozing wound
Was taken in love for me and you,
Each ounce of strength and gasping breath
Was spent to pay all sinner's debts.

Every thought and action, word and deed
Jesus performed, as He hung on the tree,
Made certain that He paved the way
To eternal life, to free US from the grave.

Every soul who looks to Christ in faith,
Is rescued from a hellish fate,
We thank you, Jesus, for gifting us,
A share of your robes, so pure and righteous.

"SEARCHING."

I'm groping in the cold, dark air,
I'm searching, for you say they're there,
Lord, I believe you, 'though I'm stressing,
When you say you've left me many blessings.
I can't see them, although I'm trying,
Is it 'cause my eyes are blurred with crying?
Maybe I'm not looking in the right place?
For I know you don't lie, and I trust in your grace.

So, I'll keep on searching in every direction,
Listen to your voice and your Holy correction,
Allow you to guide me through unchartered waters,
For you are my God, and I'm your loving daughter.
I'll not listen to all the angst that I feel,
But keep my mind open and longing eyes peeled,
Maybe in hindsight I'll find what I seek?
But for now I stay blind, with not even a peek.

But, here in the dark, I can still feel your hand,
Know you steady my feet, brace my soul, so I stand,
I'll walk on in faith, when these eyes remain useless,
Know trials help me grow and branches won't be fruitless.
So, blessings I WANT, may not be what I NEED,
Oh, please, descale my spiritual sight so I see!
I'll keep facing forward. . .pray. . .wait patiently,
For my greatest of blessings, is the friend found in Thee.

"HELLO?"

I'm calling. . .can you hear me?
Please respond. . .I'm reaching out to you,
I offer an invitation—
To be saved from sin and made brand new.
Hello down there!
Can you hear me,
Amongst the ruckus of the world?
Look up, and see me waiting,
Opened-armed, in Holy grace unfurled.

Hello to you!
Won't you reply,
To the maker of the Earth and sky?
Please answer, before it's too late,
And you have to go through Hade's gate.

Hello? Hello? . . .
I know there is no bad reception—
You choose to shun my Divine protection,
But I'll keep calling whilst you're alive,
Make sure you hear clearly, where evil does thrive.
I want us to be in Glory together,
But please be warned,
(My sin-filled spawn),
Your decision now, will last forever.

Hello. . .Hello. . .
Please heed my warning,
It's for your own sake that I'm calling,

Don't be distracted by other things,
Where selfish wants, like sirens, sing.
Why won't you look up?
Just see and feel,
Listen to your soul,
Which knows I'm real.
This is your Lord God here. . .I'm pleading.
I fear I'm wasting my Holy breath,
But remain determined to save you from death. . .
Hello? . . .
Hello? . . .

"BE PATIENT, CHILD."

Be patient in your current circumstance,
Dear child, just wait and trust in me,
For certain things in life take time,
And growth never happens immediately. . .

Flowers don't bloom in an instant,
It takes weeks for their seeds to sprout,
Their stems need strength to pierce the soil,
And grow, before the petals fan out.

When caterpillars weave their cocoons,
They need time to metamorphosize,
From grublike, wingless creatures,
Into beautiful, fluttering butterflies.

The stars wait patiently in the day,
For night, 'til they reveal their shine,
In turn, the sun waits for the dawn,
And dark to pass, 'til it has its time.

Grapes growing on their emerald vines,
Aren't plump and ready overnight,
It takes a while for fruit to sweeten,
And gather juice before it's ripe.

Bread mixed with yeast needs time to prove,
In order for the dough to rise,
Producing a high, fluffy loaf,
Which swells o'er the metal tin's sides.

Young babies in their mother's wombs
Take months of growth and preparation,
Before they're ready to be born
Into this world, following gestation.

The seasons each wait for their chance,
Which takes a calendar year before
The Spring breeze comes, then Summer's heat,
Autumn's color, and Winter's storms.

I appreciate waiting is challenging, child,
I know patience in suffering is a difficult test,
But please know that I have many reasons for this,
And at the end, you'll be wiser, stronger, and blessed.

"HELL COMES TO THE CROSS."

Hoisted into position, the beams slot and jolt,
As Christ hangs on the cross, for crimes that weren't His fault,
He's an innocent man, God made flesh, with no sin,
Takes the whole world's transgressions, crucifies them, with Him.

And next to the priests and the crowds that are jeering,
The Devil and his demons are smirking and cheering,
For they're watching and hoping that Jesus will fail,
And are goading His pain, happy, watching Him ail.

The minions of Hell have all come to the cross,
To bask in the suffering of Jesus's loss,
They revel in glee at the state of The Christ—
Crown of thorns and showing no signs of God's might.

But they cannot see what's occurring within,
For He IS The Messiah, concealed in human skin,
'though His muscles are ripping, flesh is bloody and torn,
Jesus still is our God since the day He was born.

So, there is no triumph for the powers of Hell,
For 'though His body's weak, in this frail mortal shell,
The Lord can't be contained and His power will endure,
As He hangs there, in love, conquers sin to be sure,

That all of His children will be co-heirs in Glory,
The cross won't defeat Him but be His greatest story.
Although He's in pain, more than we can imagine,
The Lamb's still a lion and is up to the challenge.

We're unable to fathom the hell Jesus faced,
As He stayed on the cross in compassion and grace,
When He drank God's wrath-cup, felt the sin pour inside,
He consumed all OUR greed, selfishness, lust and pride.

Christ is spotless and pure, shining with Heaven's light,
But was filled with our sin that stains, black as the night,
We can't comprehend how our Savior then felt,
As He fought, won, and conquered the blows evil dealt.

The Devil and demons, chief priests and the scribes
Watched, eagerly awaiting The Christ's cruel demise,
But. . .then, all these creatures shuffle nervously round,
As He cries "It Is Finished!" in victory. . .aloud.

They murmur, concerned . . . has He defeated sin?
It looks like He's lost. Could it be that He wins?
Then the great temple curtain, tears, straight down, in two,
As the earth shakes, they then quake, in their evil shoes.

A soldier pierces Jesus's side with his spear,
To check that He's dead. . .yes, He is, this is clear,
But The Devil's uneasy, not smiling or cheering,
His demons cease dancing, celebrating and jeering.

For the way that He acted, how He spoke, how He died,
Points to God's plan succeeding, when Christ was crucified,
And the demons know Scripture, and see that It was fulfilled,
Despite all the suffering, up on Calvary's hill.

There's triumphant and victory—Christ wins, there's no loss,
Even 'though Men and Satan brought hell to the cross,
Our mighty Lord Jesus took it all, in His power,
Now Good Friday is over, all the demons do cower.

For they know on the third day, Christ WILL rise again,
Mighty conqueror of death, Savior of sin and pain,
God The Son reigns supreme. . .passed the cross's great test,
Made the way for forgiveness. Thank you Jesus. . .we're blessed.

"FIX YOUR EYES ON JESUS."

Hungry eyes during salad days,
Heavy eyes in depression's haze,
Blurry eyes in anxiety's maze,
Sore eyes made by stresses' craze.

Teary eyes when times are tough,
Stinging eyes when life gets rough,
Bloodied eyes at war-cry's huff,
Hurt eyes when vicious tongues are gruff.

Damaged eyes in this world of sin,
Deceived eyes as Satan's claws dig in,
Denying eyes ponder at evil's dark grin,
Tired eyes shut down, at mental ill's din.

Aging eyes fear my weary complexion,
Stranger's eyes stare back at my mad reflection,
Confused eyes try to combat sad's infection,
Disgusted eyes balk, at harsh truth's detection.

Desperate eyes in need of rescue,
Hopeful eyes long for Redemption's view,
Yearning eyes want to be renewed,
Seeking eyes read God's promise is true.

Descaled eyes, then, are glad to see,
Enlightened eyes look up to Calvary,
Happy eyes watching Heaven with glee,
Thankful eyes see my soul flying free.

Compassionate eyes looking up to the cross,
Guilty eyes watch, as The Son pays MY cost,
Sorrowful eyes see His pain and blood-loss,
Grateful eyes watch Christ unravel sin's knots.

Joy-filled eyes at the sight of Salvation,
Awestruck eyes for The King of all nations,
Reverent eyes for The Lord of Creation,
Faithful eyes fixed upon His Holy station.

"AM I TOO LATE LORD?"

Have I left it too late Lord, to answer your call?
Will you turn your back on me, just allow me to fall?
All my life I've ignored you, as I thought I knew best,
I've been so hedonistic, but now I need rest.

For my soul is unsettled, 'though I don't know why,
So I'm bent on the floor to meet you, Lord most High.
In the past I have scoffed when there's been talk of you,
But now things have changed, and I know it's all true.

I've so much to repent for, don't know where to start,
As I'm wrinkled and aged, with a broken, old heart,
I've no right to ask for forgiveness from you,
But please know I am sorry and that my heart is true.

I fear that I won't be much use to you now,
With my creaky old bones and weather-beaten brow,
But I hope you still want me, 'though I'm battered and bruised,
I'd be honored to serve you. . .don't mind how I'm used.

I just want the peace that my soul's in your hands,
Safe and saved in Lord Jesus, Son of God, Son of Man,
So, I'm begging you Lord, on my knees I implore,
God, I ask, seek and knock, will you open the door?

"It's never too late child, to turn from your sin,
I'm so glad you knocked and will welcome you in!
I see in your heart what you profess is true,
So The Spirit will come down, to dwell inside you.

You're never too old to be part of my plan,
And I knew this would happen, before your life began!
I've been patiently waiting all these years for you,
Now I'm glad you are mine and you have been renewed.

'though you are 82, and there's not long to wait,
'til your last breath's exhaled and you're at Heaven's gate,
Rest assured your soul's safe and won't be rejected,
Through your faith in Christ Jesus you have been accepted.

So, be at peace child, knowing you're justified,
That all debts have been paid, thus I am satisfied,
You ARE fit for Heaven, regardless of age—
There's no expiry date on The Book of Life's page!"

"INSURRECTION."

Many live in the town called "Insurrection",
Where they shun Christ Jesus and the Resurrection,
Where the occupants all lead selfish lives,
Full of lust, greed, envy, lies, murder and pride.

The residing sheriff is The Devil himself,
Who swaggers around, spitting embers from Hell,
Ensuring the townsfolk stay off-piste and fallen,
Distracted and pleasured, so they don't hear God callin'.

Whilst insurrection might seem such fun,
When judgement day comes, it'll burn in The Son,
Just ask The Devil—for when HE rebelled
In Heaven, God won, and threw him down to Hell!

Promiscuity. . .drunkenness. . .'do what you like',
Is encouraged by Satan, who smiles as he bites,
But people will wake up from this evil curse,
When Jesus returns next, to harvest the earth.

Then, like Sodom and Gomorrah, The Lord sets to burn
This sinful, lost world, with the goats who won't learn,
Whilst His sheep, He will keep, safe in His Holy hand,
Who lived in Salvation whilst on this mortal land.

"Salvation's" a village, set apart from the rest,
Where the townsfolk love Jesus, show faith and are blessed,
So gladly they follow His sweet, narrow way,
Avoiding The Devil's call, to come and play.

The rules The Lord sets make for good, wholesome living,
"Salvation's" inhabitants are happy and giving,
Honesty, modesty, no murder or greed,
Loving neighbors, ensuring each has what they need.

And God provides manna, living water, fresh bread,
Daily guidance and word, redeems souls from the dead,
This town follows Jesus and drinks from His well,
The folk want for nothing and are spared wrath and Hell.

When judgement day comes, there'll be no insurrection,
For ALL will acknowledge The Christ's Resurrection,
And each knee will bow down, with no vain exception,
ALL actions explained, before God, who will question.

Then, the wheat and the chaff and the goats and the sheep,
Are set in two camps—one to burn, one to keep,
The decisions you make whilst on earth seal your fate,
So move out of The Devil's town, before it's too late.

"TWO VERY DIFFERENT BANQUETS."

When I was much younger, I took up a seat,
At The Devil's grand table, to enjoy the fine feast,
That he and this fallen world both had prepared,
And I stupidly gorged myself on what was there.

Back then I knew no better, but soon I did find
I had stomach-ache, was heavy, and quickly went blind,
I was starving, despite how much stuff I would eat,
For my plate was piled high with just transient treats.

In time, I realized both my feet had been shackled,
To this table, by thick chains the sin-master rattles,
So, now I can't leave, 'though I don't want to stay,
And I feel my soul's dying by wasting away.

The Devil distracts me by offering more,
The world feeds me lies, which makes my head so sore,
I try to break free, but these chains can't be picked,
So, I slump in my chair, feeling woeful and sick.

This table is full of other people and chatter,
Big hellhounds roam round, stealing scraps off the platters,
Some diners are happy, whilst the others just moan,
But each one of our souls lets out a helpless groan.

The Devil is satisfied and feeling amused,
The world thinks nothing's wrong, so is somewhat bemused,
I hear all the demons laugh aloud as I pour
My worries and pleas out, in a prayer, to The Lord.

But, then comes a strong wind which lets out a roar,
And Almighty Lord Jesus breaks down this hall's door,
Marches straight to the table, which He then flips aside,
Sending all the bad food flying off far and wide.

The demons go quiet, and recoil in the dark,
As The Christ breaks my chains and heals every chafe-mark,
Then I stand, take His hand, and accept when He says,
There's a place at HIS table, in Glory, instead.

The Devil protests, but he simply can't win,
'gainst the blood of The Lamb which covers all debt of sin,
The Risen Lord tells him to be quiet and go,
Back down to the depths of his dark, hellish home.

The Lord gives me strength, hope, Salvation, and peace,
Through His grace I am offered daily bread, milk, and meat,
I enjoy wine and manna 'til my soul's fit to burst,
And drink His living water, so I won't ever thirst.

The Lord's tasting good and I grow strong and wise,
I see clearly, at last, for He descales my eyes,
My heart leaps for joy and my mind's clearly fixed
On the straight path ahead, far from this realm's cheap tricks.

So, I work for The Lord throughout life, singing praise,
My faith and His succor spur me on, on tough days,
And I dream of His promise where He's saved me a seat,
Up there, waiting, in Heaven, at His great wedding feast.

"AN OVERTHINKER'S DAILY COMMUTE."

Inside my head, there tears around
A broken runaway train,
That barely holds on to the tracks,
And "Overthinker" is its name.
The carriages are paranoia, panic,
Worry and self-doubt,
And from the dawn, right through to dusk,
They chatter, clank and hoon about.

This train whistles through the stations
Named Peace, Happy, Joy and Blessed,
But stops at ones named Misery,
O.C.D., Pain and Stress.
Depression's inky, creeping tide
Does slosh its waves across the tracks,
Its driving rain is cold and numb,
And paints my train with sticky black.

Anxiety's the driver of this train
Who stokes the engine's fire,
Which means it rushes even more,
For blurring speed is its desire,
The train does screech and squeal and grind,
And barely stays upright,
It threatens to derail itself,
And plunge down where there is no light.

The steam flies out in constant streams,
And tired lights fade and flicker,

I fear this train will shake apart,
As wheels just race along much quicker.
Each iron rivet's working loose,
I hear the creaking of the funnel,
Every inch is under strain,
When it roars through depression's tunnel.

In desperation I cry out,
Up to The Lord above,
And ask Him to come rescue me,
As trust His mercy, grace and love,
In great compassion He responds,
And comes to ease the engine's screams,
He listens to my woes and stress,
And helps me, then, to let off steam.

He reassures He's in control,
And if I pause, calm, focus, clear,
I'll keep His Heaven's view in mind,
And realize that He's always near.
When I submit myself to God,
I'm instantly less stressed,
And my engine pulls up calmly to
The station of The Lord called "Blessed."

"UNEARTHING THE RAINBOW."

I'll unearth the rainbow from the dirt,
Buried deep beneath my trials and hurt,
Where worries, pain and sorrows make
Its hopeful colors fade and wait.
But I will hunt and dig them out,
Go round the Devil, past self-doubt,
I'll shovel, 'though woe's water gushes,
And heartache's tears, that bring hot flushes.

I'll unearth the rainbow to set it free,
And find the bliss God's promised me,
His consolations are always found,
Even when joy's buried, so deep underground.
You cannot have growth, when you haven't felt pain,
Likewise, there is no rainbow, where there isn't rain.
God's bands of compassion, love, manna and grace,
Are always there, waiting, to be found by faith.

It's our job to unearth the myriad of blessings,
Throughout the mud-slides of life's trials and stressing,
For our God is loving and a God of true hope,
Gives compassion and succor, to help us to cope.
So, never give up, or put your shovel down,
Think that there is no rainbow and only gloom's brown,
This great technicolor is just waiting to shine,
And it IS always there—all you need is some time.

"DO NOT FEAR TROUBLED WATERS."

Don't fear the troubled waters that are lapping round your toes,
I understand the worry and the stress inside that grows,
But you don't need to fret my child, nor try to run and hide,
For I won't let the tide of woe consume those who are mine.

Don't fear the troubled waters that are lapping round your knees,
And please remember that I always hear your heartfelt pleas,
Don't feel unsettled that these waves are nudging round your legs,
For I will keep you steady, calm the mounting thoughts of dread.

Don't fear the troubled waters that are swirling round your waist,
That make your heartbeat frantically and mind whirr-up to race,
For I can reassure you that you won't get swept away,
And in my mighty armor, you will live to fight another day.

Don't fear the troubled waters that are swelling to your shoulders,
That pull and drag and jostle, create fear that makes you colder,
For my hand is upon you and you can relax in me,
As I made planet earth, the sun and moon and stars and sea.

Don't fear the troubled waters that now eddy round your chin,
That try to shield your face from me and tempt you then to sin,
Just point your head and heart straight up, towards my home in Glory,
And trust that I will guide you through this trial in your life's story.

Don't fear the troubled waters—I'll not let them grab and take you,
Don't get me wrong, it will be hard, as struggles try to break you,
But know my child, I have you in my mighty hand of grace,
And I'll hold and encourage you, through pain and woes that chase.

Don't fear the troubled waters, for they're all within my hand,
And I will send them back in my great timing and command,
For now, there's lessons to learn, as you think, react and swim,
You're gaining wisdom, strength and Holy understanding deep within.

Don't fear the troubled waters, for my Spirit lives in you,
And HE can never be consumed by anything of worldly view,
The Spirit, 'though invisible, makes you my soldier, fierce and strong,
And keeps you upright, walking true, throughout the times when things
seem wrong.

Don't fear the troubled waters, for in time they'll make you see,
That they've made you a fighter and have brought you closer towards me,
So rest assured, my precious one, throughout your mortal days,
During all your troubled waters, I'll still give you cause to sing my praise.

"WE'LL GET THROUGH THIS TOGETHER."

Just take one small step at a time,
I'll not let you slip, for thou art mine,
I know this path is difficult,
And you're bound to stumble. . .that's not your fault.

Just do your best and know I'm here,
I'm The Shepherd who keeps my sheep near,
When you tire, I'll help you pick up the pace,
Carry you, so you rest, in my mercy and grace.

Just remember I share in your sufferings too,
Lean on me for support and I WILL see you through,
I know you're confused, stressed-out and feel weak,
For I hear the emotions you can't bear to speak.

I'm sorry you have to face all of these battles,
And fight through the storms that leave peace of mind rattled,
Remember that I can calm all with my hand,
When I won't, I'll support you, 'til we reach dry land.

And sometimes, in hindsight, you're taught troubled waters
Are needed to help you grow strong as you ought-to,
For faith's only tested by tragedy's kiss,
But remember I'm with you, walking flames in the furnace.

In future you'll see like a phoenix you'll rise
From these ashes and hot tears you currently cry,
For I'll grant you wisdom, endurance and wings,
And gift your soul stamina, for whatever life brings.

I do this for every child that I call mine,
Who I've saved from the dark and redeemed for all time,
Recall, I walked this earth in flesh as The Christ,
And felt all sorts of pain, so I KNOW it's not nice.

Listen out to your soul which still sings out with glee,
Flex your faith, realize that you can't break in ME,
And although you are weary and scared to the bone,
Just remember "I AM" and that you're NOT alone.

"NO POWER HIGHER."

You WILL find forgiveness in The Christ,
So, don't be ashamed to lay your all,
At His Holy feet and the mighty cross,
Where He conquered sin and made it fall.

Trust that there's no transgression's pile,
Too large that it could overcome,
The power of Christ upon the cross,
For "It is finished," and this war is won.

For nothing's taller than the cross,
And nothing's wider than its reach,
Its shadow covers all the Earth,
And this Holy tree roots run so deep.

Its high-top touches Heaven's sky,
Its horizontal beams are arms,
Just waiting to embrace you,
And rescue souls from any sort of harm.

Darkness now crawls on its knees,
Satan loses and all evil cowers,
For the cross is the symbol of Calvary,
Where God The Son unleashed His awesome power.

There is nothing that's higher than The Lord,
And there's no-one equal, or above,
Incomparable and indestructible,
He rose from the dead and reigns with love.

The serpent's head is kicked and squashed,
Sin's curse is lifted. . .chains undone,
Death's not the end, just a journey,
Thanks to the cross and the mighty risen Son.

SECTION TWO

All poems written as collaborations between
Suzanne Newman & Michael Grgich—MAG.

"SAND-DUNES."

There's challenging and shifting sand, beneath my weak and weary feet,
My soles are cracked and blistered and my eyes wince in the glaring heat,
Although I try to march along, it's hard to keep a steady pace,
When ground I'm forced to walk upon, unnerves and moves me off my place.
I try to find the cornerstone—The Rock on which I know I'm blessed,
I'm thirsting for God's manna and I need respite on Jesus' chest,
But endless seem these dunes of pain, that grow and change throughout life's trials,
I can't see anything but sand, and sorrow that goes on for miles.

I dig with bare and burning hands, in scorching rays that won't relent,
But all I find is layers of sand, and now my mind is parched is bent,
These gritty grains do chafe the skin and give no nutrients or shade,
I need The Lord to pull me through this testing desert, trials have made.
My own reserves are dwindling and the will to live is fading fast,
I throw myself upon God's grace, which has served me so well in the past,
"Dear Lord", I cry out in distress, "Please send me help in this wilderness,
For I am worn. . .my hope is torn. . .I'm feeling woeful and distressed.
I trust you, Lord, I know there's always Holy lessons to be learned,
But, right now, all I feel is pain, where this shifting sand has caused me burns".

There is no shelter, no escape,
So, in the desert sun I bake,
There is no comfort to be found,
Only hellfire, all around.
So, I dig my hands into the sand,
Screaming: "Lord, I'm just a man!

85

Christ, please take my shaking hand"!
As I'm swallowed down by life's demands,
Time to embrace my faith and take a stand.
So, as sand crystals whip at me,
Blinding these eyes so I can't see,
I grow within the soul in me,
Feel the warmth under my Christ's great wing.

Trials are trials and will always be there. . .I can never escape that human
fate, Just hope my Savior hears my prayers, before it's finally too late.
So two knees bend and two hands clasp, a soul fills up with Holy light,
I pray to God through this sandstorm, that He will hold me tight tonight.
"And so I pray . . .
That your grace covers me today,
A servant to your righteous hand,
I bow to all that you command."

And, so, I cease my struggling. . .admit I can't cope on my own,
Submit myself to God completely, whatever ill winds come to blow,
The Lord gives me these sand-dunes, in His wisdom, and He'll pull me
through,
I sit. . .await direction. . .have faith God will show me what to do.

And when I stop scooping the sands, with human hands, and use the soul,
I find Christ's living water, which refreshes and is nice and cold,
It bubbles up from underground, and soon I find this spring has turned
Into a massive pool of life, amongst the desert lands that burn.
So, God provides me hope and succor, in this harsh, bleak wilderness,
Creates a calm oasis, in which I can pray and shield and rest,
He plants me firm upon The Rock, which I find now amongst the sand,
Which stops my feet from slipping, whilst He steadies me with Holy hand.
I realize that God's always there, but I have to dig deep sometimes,
There's always gold within the soul, if I put the effort in and mine.
Christ is my refuge in the storms, and hope and manna in life's dunes,
He stops my soul from burning up, for is the shade in heat of noon.

And, so, now faith replenished and with renewed strength in God's good
grace,
I set off on my journey. . .now conquering each sand-dune I must face.

In every life, at some point, we face trials that we must weather,
In every life each one of us at some time must brave our own desert,
But the sand of the dunes can be soft and comforting,
When God provides place for your footing,
If you believe in The Trinity,
Life water of Christ will be flowing free
From every sand dune. . .if you just believe . . .

"PILLARS."

So, the two of us write our souls to you,
Both tender and massing misery,
Many times we do join forces,
To bring to you our reverent knees,
We are not saints, nor prophets,
Merely Christians writing, with Christ inside,
Humans, no longer afraid to preach our eternal love to Jesus Christ.
Pillars of love,
Pillars of faith,
Building pillars to God, make no mistake!

So, with our words, not only do we praise. . .we teach,
We like to dare to hope?
Despair transforms to love,
Giving all the glory to Lord Jesus, Christ above.
Pillars being built up high,
Readied under our Savior's eye.

We're not pillars of the community,
Just standing in Christ, faithfully,
Worshipping continually,
Realize our place, so humbly.
Give thanks in all humility,
Praise Jesus, Savior, reverently,
Following Him eternally,
Our souls and hearts with Him completely.

For we stand firm, as pillars of The Lord, in His amazing grace,
Made strong because of Jesus, we stretch high to try to touch His face,

He makes us solid. . .steadfast. . .and our base can withstand any shocks,
For it is planted, built upon, His Cornerstone and Holy Rock.
Our mortal minds and bodies may be crumbling into chalky dust,
The powder's shaking off our pillars, as we're destroyed by sin and lust,
This world may make us crack up, leave us trembling at our very core,
The Devil and our selfish side, can make our struggles hard and raw,
Life's trials send us earthquakes and the winds of change can gust around,
But nothing knocks us down, because the promise of The Lord is sound.

For God is ever faithful and His grace and power know no end,
He never lets His children break, regardless how life makes us bend,
He is our solid concrete, wrapped around a rod of strongest steel,
His love is omnipresent, everlasting, tangible and real.

Christ's blood and righteous victory is running through our columned-veins,
Comforting and strengthening, when we are weary. . .teary. . .drained,
The Father listens to our prayers when we cry out, plead and complain,
The Holy Spirit makes us brave, and roars throughout our redeemed grain,
Our Triune God gives succor, armor coating, in His awesome name,
So, we can withstand anything. . .no matter how brutal the pain.

When God creates and sustains us,
Not even Samson's strength could push us down!
We won't be turned to pillars of salt,
Like Lot's wife, who swayed and turned around.
In God we stand upright and firm,
And focus on our Heaven's goal,
Knowing that we'll get there,
For He underpins our very souls.

Pillars come in many shapes and sizes—every color, every culture, every
creed,
Your own pillar's construction begins the exact moment your soul's
conceived,
All our pillars are built strong by God. . .forged of many righteous things,
Constructed of Divine materials and built by the work of angel's wings.

Sands of Faith form the structure, to support the hard steel core of love,
Crafted bricks of hope surround it, ordained with devotions offered to God above.
A hole remains at its base—a gateway for your soul to find its home inside,
Then the finger of God graces the hole, to seal your soul so safe inside.
Your new pillar descends from Heaven, the instant that your new flesh is conceived,
The pillared home of your soul then bonds with your new-born Earthly being.
So, we ALL are pillars of the Lord, loved and built by His mighty hand,
But it is up to US as mortal children of Christ, to make sure that our pillars stand.

"TIME-MACHINE."

So many days I pause to dream,
How grand and glorious it would be
To have and control a time machine—
Go back in time and fix past me.

So many days I've sat and wept,
Drenched in the sin I can't forget,
Back in time blindly, in the current, swept,
If I could travel back, I could correct.

So many days I've lived for me,
Blinded by sin, I could not see,
I ran from God as He reached for me,
All could be reversed with a Time Machine.

For, what if I'd met God before?
Before bad choices chafed me raw?
Would life have left me quite so sore?
If, all along, He was at my core.

For that's one day I DON'T regret –
The day Lord Jesus and I met,
When I accepted, He paid all debt,
Hence my path to Hell could be reset.

I recall tears streaming from my eyes,
When I knelt before The Risen Christ,
As I repented and told no lies,
He heard and loved me, through each sad sigh.

But suddenly, it dawns on me,
If I really had a time machine,
And went back to adjust my scene,
Would I be the person today, I see?

For all the wrongs and sin I've done,
Lead down this road to meet The Son,
And suddenly, if that WERE all gone,
Would I fully appreciate all He's done?

So, maybe I wouldn't change a thing,
If I found myself driving a time machine,
For the good and bad and everything,
Means that I was ripe to meet The King.

So many regrets and many bad scenes,
So many nightmares I wish I could unsee,
But past is past, and dreams are just dreams,
None can be undone without a time machine.

Time moves fast and the world will spin,
And we are all caught here, in the mean,
'though none of us have a time machine,
Brethren, keep faith. . . all's just as it should be.

"WAVES."

Most things in life will come in waves –
Love and broken hearts will ebb and flow,
Emotions constant movement can be raging high, or gentle low,
Struggles cause great tempests—their tsunamis crash upon our shore,
Stress, confusion, and regret, dizzy us into a whirlpool's core.
Waves of joy and happiness lap fleetingly through season's tides,
Whilst killer swells and sorrow's foam try to drag us down, to drown inside.

The white caps raid the shoreline, as indecision takes our minds,
The waves are licking and taking sand, reminiscing what's been left behind,
We fight through our waves every day, managing the changing tides,
But somehow find ourselves still treading water, in our choppy minds.
But there is one that you can find,
To tame the seas whipping your side,
A bright, and brilliant shining light –
Our Lord and Savior Jesus Christ.
If you are brave and allow it,
HE will tame the waves.

For The Son of God can calm the storms,
Command "Be still!" the waves that roar,
And He will take our hand across
The troubled-water's foam and froth.
And waves can't swamp His mighty power,
Even when tsunami's loom and tower,
And 'though we may feel it's all too much,
God helps us through, with His grace-filled touch.

We won't sink, 'though we eddy round,
For The Lord ensures we cannot drown,
When churning waves like lions, growl,
The Holy Spirit exceeds this sound,
Reminds us we're on solid ground,
For Christ's The Rock where peace is found.

Then, as if like magic, feet can rise above the dense and swirling surf,
When a Holy, helping hand is offered, and a soothing numb embraces our
hurt.
On top of the waves, we can gaze into The Savior's loving eyes,
Which give eternal wealth, open-up blind eyes, making our joyous tears rise.

We're aware that it often causes some waves,
When we stand up and witness to how Jesus saves,
We've been mocked and threatened, put down and provoked,
Had haters come at us, saying God is a joke,
But Christ gives us strength, love and will to press on,
Against this rising tide, so aggressive and strong.

We're not perfect, just sinners who've been saved in grace,
We are God's humble servants, not saintly nor great,
We cannot make huge waves in this wide, wicked world,
But we hope to make ripples with the words that we swirl,
That make other people think about our great Lord,
Who's grace freely flows, like a vast waterfall,
Who's majesty cascades, reigns supreme over all,
Who's promises are true, shining like faithful swords.

Battling tides to claim our right
To be with The Almighty Jesus Christ,
Waves crash about, but we don't lose sight,
For souls in Him, will win any fight.

Jesus saves. . . so we'll conquer waves.

"MASK OF SORROW."

Hello world . . . here I am, broken by my very own hand,
I feel the darkness creeping in—depression, coming to feed into my sin,
A head that's all a cluster, lost in all the fluster,
Happiness seems an empty offer, sadness seeps, and drips all over.
It's not at all a choice of mine, these dark thoughts that fill, invade my mind,
I have tried over and over, time after time, to stop this force stalking my life,
I run, but I can't get away, the tar has me stuck in the thick of its decay,
Afraid, I'm scared, my life astray, my only shelter is to kneel and pray,
Hope Christ will find it in His grace, to answer what I desperately ask. . .
"Please Jesus, temper my depression, please Christ remove my sorrow's mask.

I yearn for sheer, blessed, sweet relief,
For under this mask, it's so hard to breathe,
I'm tired all day, but at night cannot sleep,
I'm flagging with the nagging of depression's bleak bleat.
Each day's the same—mind groggy with grief,
Heart's heavy, like it's made of block concrete,
Sorrows pain claws and digs in deep,
Whilst eyes are blind with the tears I weep.
As I struggle along, gritting aching teeth,
On this long, hard road of life, so steep,
My faith-filled base is strong beneath,
For soul still keeps the cross in reach.

I come before you fractured, Lord, wearing this dark mask of pain and
sorrow,
I'm nervous to discard it, as it's familiar and underneath, I'm left hollow,
This life has dealt me many blows, plus I'm suffocated by sin's curse,

I fear I'm drowning in this black, whilst I'm starved of peace and die of thirst—
There's "Water, water everywhere, but not a drop to drink!"
Depression's rising tide is toxic and is pleased to watch contentment sink.

My soul's still light, 'though its brightness dims,
My praise is lack-luster to sing any hymns,
My prayers are full of this silent woe,
For it's hard to speak where depression does grow.
The blackness swells and chokes all joy,
Desperate currents carry it way past the buoys,
Into troubled waters, so dark and so deep,
'til I've drifted quite far from The Shepherd's safe keep.

Can anyone see this pain under my mask?
Does anyone care? Will somebody ask?
Sorrows iron-out all laughter lines,
Which whirlpool down in depression's tides.

It's all a fantasy, merely a facade, these feelings of me at odds with God,
But I'm a human, I own human flaws, I can't predict what pains may flog,
So the tar quickens. . .it thickens. . .depression takes my soul I'm not a person,
Not a human, I'm just a chunk of useless road, I cannot believe in me.
The mask on me is way too tight, but I want, I need, I crave, a life. . .
A happiness through Jesus Christ.
But this mortal world grabs onto me, ten thousand hands just pull me down,
On a mind already weakened, honestly, where is my salvation found?
God tells me that He tends to me, "Child your soul is mine,"
But so often with my depression, I choose to cast that truth aside.

For, in the mask of sorrow, it's so hard to see the Holy light,
Images and thoughts are twisted, blinding me with lies and fright,
But underneath my soul's unhampered, sees and trusts my loving Lord,
And knows that He is by my side, 'though struggles rage and darkness claws.

My soul trusts in God's wisdom, knows that 'though this trial may test and burn,
Before this mask is lifted, there are vital lessons I must learn,
And even when I do not feel it, God, (in grace), is always near,
It's just that when pain's shouting loud, He's often difficult to hear.

Behind every mask there lives a heart 'though, and a light-craving, happy soul,
Behind the tears of misery, lives a strong person trying to let sadness go,
Behind the porcelain, behind the paper, behind the shield that you have to hold,
Stands a Light to shatter darkness—greatest defense against depression's woes.

So, I will walk this road of life,
Content to feel my way by faith,
Knowing God supports and guides,
Despite the mask of sorrow on my face.

Sadness and sorrow CAN be erased,
When these masks are lifted by our Savior Jesus's grace.

"TREASURE."

I know I'm nothing special,
And I'm definitely nothing grand,
But still The Lord upholds me,
And cares for me with a gracious hand.
I struggle with life daily,
And have many weaknesses and flaws,
But somehow, I'm still precious,
Valued, wanted, and loved by The Lord!

For some great unknown reason
God includes me in His Holy plan,
I'm baffled and can't comprehend,
Am grateful, but don't understand!
I see I have such little worth,
But God views me as priceless,
And 'though I'm hard upon myself,
His promises reassure and bless.

Many verses tell me in Scripture,
That I'm a wonderous treasure to behold,
For I have been crafted in the image of
Our one and true Almighty Lord!
He finds the worth in me, that I alone fight to see,
He fills my heart and soul with love and hope,
He offers me a blissful eternity,
Warm and safe, like a Holy treasure-trove.

Even when I doubt myself in this life,
His hand reaches for me from the clouds,

To give me the strength to tackle my trials,
The courage to rise up when I've been knocked down.
And as He tends to me, He teaches me,
To have faith, to have love, to have hope,
So, I thank Jesus on my knees daily,
For letting His Holy wisdom freely ebb and flow.

And this to me is priceless—
Worth much more than all the world's fine treasure—
To have Salvation in The Christ
Is my soul's everlasting, one true pleasure.
For souls make no requests for diamonds,
Fine cars, houses, gold, or jewels,
As these won't bring us comfort,
And have no value to anyone but a fool.

We can't drag money with us
When The Reaper takes our curtain call,
Whilst we're busy grabbing Earthly wealth,
Our mortal souls are sure to fall,
Into the pit where Satan dwells,
Who's busy smelting lots of coins,
To bribe us poor, weak humans with—
Lure us into Hell and roast our loins.

But you can't buy a saved soul,
One who's been bought by the blood of Christ,
For we know peace is treasure,
So, we're happy living in The Light.
And Heaven is our promised prize,
The Spirit is our precious gift,
And God's companionship through life
Brings us priceless comfort, strength, and lift.

To hear The Shepherd's loving voice,
Is the sweetest music to my ears,

To feel His love and compassion,
Helps my faith through trials and fills heart with cheer.
You cannot put a price upon
God's ever-present care and grace,
And if The Devil were to try,
I'd laugh right in his fallen face!

So. . .keep your Earthly 'treasures' of greed,
My treasure is gifted from The Divine,
My soul bathes within a Holy wealth,
My Faith is loyal, strong, and primed.
Riches do not cease life's bitter trials,
Nor does wealth relinquish pain,
But a Heavenly treasure is offered to all
Through our Savior, sweet Jesus's name.

The reward is there for me, if I seek it,
Renouncing all my Earthly greed,
The eternal treasure of true paradise
Can be seen clearly from my bended knees.
The Devil will print cash and treasure maps,
And tempt weak mortal minds with pleasures,
Staying strong in Faith, I keep eyes on the prize,
Realizing I am loved. . .I am Heaven's treasure!

"DEBT."

I've been running up the total,
With each bad decision made,
The debt I've built ever since birth,
Is following me to the grave.

The Devil's face is buried in the ledger,
Keeping track of every charge within
My debt, growing exponentially,
The total swelling with every sin.

He grins and gets his ink-pen out,
The cartridge is filled up with blood,
From all the lost souls he has claimed,
Who gnash and wail in their tear-flood.

The Devil seems quite happy,
More than satisfied I've done enough
To warrant my place down in Hell,
Where punishment is dark and tough.

"Oh deary me!" he chuckles,
With a gleeful glint inside his eyes,
"You've racked-up a long list of sin. . .
Please check the invoice I've supplied!"

My eyes widen in disbelief,
My worried soul drops to my feet,
Staring at the bill presented me,
I've much to pay. . .such a long receipt.

With desperation to the core,
Quick inhale. . .I take a breath,
I drop my faith-filled knees to floor,
And lightning-quick clasp hands to chest.

I rest my mind. . .I close my eyes. . .
And with all I am I pray to Christ,
For only He can make it right,
And protect my soul from a nasty fright.

I've nothing with which to pay my bill –
For no money, diamonds, or gold,
Can match the priceless value
Of someone's immortal soul.

The Devil smirks quite mockingly,
As sees my desperate state,
He stokes my fire-pit down in Hell,
Convinced of my forsaken fate.

He lifts his pen and licks his lips,
Then moistens the red pointed tip,
Proceeds to mark a guilty tick
By each sin on my judgement list.

But. . .before The Devil finishes,
Christ Jesus rushes to my aid,
Picks up the reem of charges,
And removes the ticks that Satan made.

An eyebrow raising to The Savior,
Satan demands the bill needs paid,
But Christ pricked His finger on the thorns,
So His blood washes the sin away.

He then goes down my shameful list
And next to each charge, puts a cross,
Displays for everyone to see,
That HE takes it all and covers the cost.

I can feel my soul lighten,
I can feel my burdens die,
I can feel the shelter of The Shepherd,
I can feel the power of Jesus Christ.

The charges within the ledger
Then quickly start to dissipate,
One by one, becoming paid in full,
As sin by sin, they are erased.

I look to Jesus, trembling,
Thankful for His Holy touch,
Bow my humble head before Him,
And then offer Him my love.

"My child", He says in compassionate grace,
"I heard your prayers said on your knees,
Accept your declaration of faith,
And believe all your repentant pleas.

Do you accept me in your heart?
Would you like to come and dwell with me?
Just say the word and I shall shepherd
You into my care for eternity."

I proclaim, "I do, my Lord!
My life's forever in your keep,
I want to walk the narrow way,
My heart and soul lay at your feet."

Jesus smiles a beaming smile,
His flowing robes are white as snow,
He whispers in a loving voice,
"Your debt's now paid, my child. Let's go."

"BEEN LOOKING."

Been looking for so many things, I've looked in so many places,
Looking into life about this Earth, looking in so many of Man's faces,
I've been looking for, and thought I could find, my very own dreams,
But mind and heart and mortal life told me to forget about those things.

Been looking for answers, been searching for some righteous paths,
Been frantically trying to find, faith once forgotten in this world's aftermath,
Been looking, searching, seeking, exploring, I have been looking for what-
ever's more,
Been looking to show that darkness even once inside, can still be removed
from a torn soul's door.

Been looking, searching, everywhere, for the elusive thing called "peace,"
I've heard it calms all troubles and can make even mountainous fears cease,
Been looking all over this mad, sad, world, for something to fill this empty
hole,
I have within my deepest core, for my broken soul longs to be whole.

Been looking for satisfaction, distraction, at the bottom of a whiskey glass,
In pills and drugs and casual sex, but all these highs so quickly pass,
Been looking, but yet have failed to find, the thing that my soul's searching
for,
I feel a hunger and thirst within, which I cannot stop and don't know the
cure.

Been looking for pieces of myself, that have been broken off and lost,
Some pieces I choose just to forget, other pieces paid for sin I wrought,

But a single puzzle piece remains missing—my jigsaw's left with a glaring hole,
I have been looking for the solution to the riddle, the way to make whole the portrait of my soul.

Been looking at my full bank account and the nice food I have on my plate,
But my soul's not interested in this—just cries with so much to contemplate,
Been looking everywhere I think of. . .desperately groping around in cold, dark, dirt,
'til the hole inside my woeful soul whispers, "The answer isn't found down here on Earth!"

Been looking at all of time's strings, been looking for just a single clue,
Anything that helps me see the light, with eyes open anew,
I've been growing weary of my query, and all of the righteous love I crave,
Time to look deep within myself, time to be unafraid, time to be brave.

Been looking deep within the core of me, and when I do a bright light shines,
A comfort calms my mind and heart, and a vision of pure love fills my eyes,
I see everything I have been looking for starts in the center of my soul,
As this very love draws my mortal eyes up to God's throne and Jesus's home.

Been looking. . .but not looking UP. . .and not noticing Heaven's wonderous skies,
But now I do, it's a revelation! And see that this is where my answer lies,
Been looking for eons, so it seems, but now finally The Truth has called my name,
Jesus vows to make my soul-hole whole, and His grace and love replace my sin and shame.

What I've been looking for, searching for, questing for, throughout my broken life,
Has always been right here with me, warming and teaching my soul from deep inside!

No longer looking for what is not missing, no more empty cravings, no more chasing dreams,
I found soul pleasure that I treasure. . .I found Jesus is forever with me.

And Lord Jesus Christ's acceptance, forgiveness, Redemption, and gracious sweet Salvation,
Leave no more gaps within this mortal being, for soul-holes are filled in by The Maker of Creation,
And The Holy Spirit's presence means everything inside is permanently full of light,
So now I have found what I what it is I've been looking for, thanks to The Lord's amazing love and Might.

"IMAGINE. . ."

Imagine you are Noah, contacted by the one true Lord,
Would you share that encounter with others, would you believe it in your core?
Told the worlds about to change, and the fate of it lies on you!
If you were Noah, in the instant, what ever would you choose?
Told he needs to build, what has never been built, a new accomplishment for Man,
Told he needs to gather two of all land-based life, Noah honored this command.
So, with ridicule from kinsman, and shame thrown from those who do not see,
Noah planned the work and crafted the craft as our loving Lord decreed.

Imagine you are dear old Job—a Godly, true, and blameless man,
You had the things that he had—money, kin, and herds, and lots of land,
It would be easy, would it not, to have faith and praise God's great name,
When you have everything you want. . .but what about on woe-filled days?
If God changes your circumstance, and The Devil comes to test and hurt,
Would you still hold on to your faith defiantly, or give up and desert?
Would you survive sackcloth and ashes days? Would you stick with God in deepest grief?
Would you still stand up and testify in front of mocking friends who have no belief?

Imagine you are David, tending your flock, keeping your sheep,
As an army of your enemies, upon your kingdom creeps,
A titan of a warrior, sent by the dark to claim the crown,
Even the strongest in the kingdom cowering, no bravery to be found.

Are you strong enough, in your faith? Would you stand behind God and
that flimsy sling?
When facing what seems insurmountable, what seems like sure defeat, so
grim?
David stood tall and confident, and through God's grace conquered what
he stood before,
If you were David facing your own titans, would your faith be as sure?

Imagine you are Daniel, facing vast pressure from society to conform,
Would you fear and give in to their wants? Or would you stay faithful to
our one true Lord?
Would you pray to and trust in God when pushed into the hungry lion's den?
Would you have faith in His wise ways, or would you cower at the hands of
men?
Imagine seeing your three friends standing up for God when everybody
else bows,
Would you join them, and defend them? Would you still love God, or
would you panic now?
Would you be worried about the heat of the fiery furnace's fearsome flames?
Or would you know that God is with you there, as you call for strength in
His mighty name?

Imagine you are Abraham and told to sacrifice your first-born son,
Would you faithfully conceded, to what God decreed, or would you turn
and run?
Could you coax him up the mountain, could you still look into his mother's
eyes?
Could you trust that God is just? Do you have that strength inside?
Asked to give away what you treasure most, without a reason why,
Could you wipe the tears from your eyes, could you lift the dagger high in
the sky?
Would you trust that God is just, and He would stop your knife-wielding
hand?
Would your faith be as granite strong, just as our father Abraham?

Imagine you were Simeon, would you be sure of the promise God had made,
That someday you would see The Messiah before you died and laid in your
mortal grave.
Would you trust what The Holy Spirit revealed? Would you wait patiently
upon The Good Lord's time?
Would you be faithfully led and guided, and respond appropriately to this
gift Divine?
Imagine you were Simeon, going excitedly into the temple courts,
To meet and greet Joseph and Mary as they presented the babe, as was
custom of the law,
Would you gaze in love, delight, and awe, at the living miracle before your
aging eyes?
Would you thank God for keeping His promise to you, and for birthing
The Savior of all Mankind?

Imagine you were Moses, living lush, over your kin enslaved,
Would you stand up against the Pharaoh? In your heart are you that brave?
Guided only by a bush and faith, like Moses, would you break the chains?
And become the shepherd of a nation, leading a flock out of slavery.
Would you pray to God to help you and believe in the help yet to come?
Would your faith guide you steady through the water that does not run?
When the desert seems so vast and endless, does your faith dry up as well?
Or like Moses does your faith guide you, to the land promised to Israel?

Imagine you were Joeseph, loved and favored by your father too much,
So all your brothers hated you and showed disdain with each word, deed,
and touch,
Would you despise them in return? Would you wish great harm upon them?
Would you be confused and angry when they sold you to some merchant
men?
Would you trust God in your darkest hour? Would you trust that all was in
His plan?
Would you keep the faith when tested and falsely accused when living in
Pharaoh's land?
In time, Joseph held a position of power and had authority to help his
brothers or not,

If you were him, would you pay their hatred back? Or would you be forgiv-
ing and compassionate in the name of God?

Imagine you are John, your faith is strong, you're bathing reborn souls,
Washing those who crave it, preaching the Lord's gospel,
How would you react in the moment, when The Son of Man stood in the
stream?
And told you that it fell to you to wash HIS already Godly-soul obediently
clean!
Could you humble yourself as John did, would you accept your role to play?
When you feel you are unworthy, but God sees it a different way.
If Jesus came before you and asked you to baptize Him, 'though He had no
sin,
Could you claim a humble faith, as John did, and through your obedience
could you baptize HIM?

Imagine you are Saul—a ruthless persecutor of the Christian faith,
Imprisoning people near and far who dare to trust in Jesus's power and grace,
Imagine you are on the road to Damascus when suddenly you are stunned
and fall
From your horse, onto the dirt road, blinded by The Light so you can't see
at all.
Imagine if everything you thought you knew to be true was changed in an
instant,
When God The Son confronts you, speaks directly to you and you know
you cannot stand against.
Imagine suddenly having your once blind eyes descaled so then you can see,
And you start your Christian life reborn, as Paul, with a passion for fearless
ministry.

Imagine you are the fisherman Simon, scraping the reef to feed your clan,
And the fish seem to avoid the net, when a stranger comes and says, "I'll
make you a fisher of man!"
How do you react when He casts the nets, and those nets are pulled in filled?
Do you see the gift before you? Do you see our Savior's will?

Imagine your name was changed to Peter, and a gracing was given to your soul,
To carry out our Savior's will, and still bleed the gospel after He is killed,
Would your pencil have the power to scribe? Would your soul have the strength to testify?
If you were Simon/Peter, would your faith so readily accept the one true Christ?

Imagine you're a Samaritan woman, fetching water in the noon-day sun,
A stranger sitting by the well talks to you and seems to know everything you've ever done!
Would you be alarmed and run away? Or would you stop and listen to what He says,
When He explains about living water, never thirsting again, and how He can leave you blessed.
Imagine The Messiah was talking to you! How would you feel and what would your reaction be?
Would you disrespect and reject Him? Or would you run excitedly to tell everyone that you see?
Would you realize you're unworthy, of The Christ's attention, time, love, redemption, and grace?
Would your heart and soul leap for joy and would hopeful, peaceful tears pour down your face?

Imagine you're Mary, a young woman just tending to the things you need,
And an angel appeared before you, saying, "The Good Lord sent me. . ."
Told you "You are going to bear a child, 'though, you will remain un-touched by man,
And HE will be the Savior of all of life and all of Man!" How would YOU react to that command?
How could you tell your beloved fiancé, that you carry a Divine seed?
Would your faith be strong enough to test he would trust you and believe?
And when he did, within yourself, would your faith be strong enough to carry on,
Would and could you bear the burden, of being the Son of Man's Earthly Mum?

Imagine you are Samson, blessed by God with super strength, would you
Judge right to use it wisely, in obedience to God's will and view?
Would you trust God for your stamina, and direction, or would you be
tempted to stray,
When faced by your own "Deliah", which then makes you really weak in so
many ways.
If you were Samson, blinded, overwhelmed by betrayal and your hateful foes,
And found yourself imprisoned, feeling regretful, scared, and quite alone,
Would you be able to humble yourself, and beg for mercy and strength as
Samson did?
Would you be able to stand, prove your faith is true, showing the power of
God cannot be hid?

Imagine you are Stephen, a servant of God, spreading HIS word,
Embraced by the believers, others casting you out as absurd,
But through faith you keep your heart strong and preach to reach out for
God's hand,
Despite when you were shunned and convicted, by the false righteous hand
of man.
How would you feel, starring at the stones, that are soon to be thrown?
Could you post and take the hits? Knowing in your heart your soul is
atoned?
Would you be as brave as Stephen was, would you look death straight in
the eye?
Would your faith be strong enough, like Stephen, to carry you on home to
Jesus Christ?

Imagine you're a rich man, who comes to Jesus with an important question,
You want to gain eternal life, what must you do? Does He have a suggestion?
You've followed God's commandments all your life and wonder what you
lack,
When Jesus tells you sell all you own, give it to the poor and it's a fact
That you will have treasure in Heaven then, 'though this greedy world will
think you mad,
Give it up, give it all and then follow me! But the rich man turned away so
sad,

For He loved His wealth more than anything. Could YOU give up everything to be with Christ The King?
Do you value Him more than earthly wealth and the false security these things bring?

Imagine you're a simple sinner. . .for that's all that any mortal ever is,
Would you stay lost, helpless, and bound for Hell, or would you ask Lord Jesus if you could be His?
Imagine if He offered you a way to be cleansed from your deep, deadly sin,
Would you accept this grace-filled gift, repenting upon your knees, in faith through Him?
Imagine if you said no. . .no to the opportunity for soul Salvation and peace,
Denied The Christ and carried on living your life exactly how you please,
Imagine you've no support or guidance from The Triune God in your troubled times,
How lonely and frightening life would be, followed by The Reaper coming for you with a doomed, dark scythe.

"FLY ON THE WALL."

If I was a fly on the wall of my life, what would that fly say about my soul?
The scenes that it had witnessed, the stories my soul told?
If I was a fly on the wall, watching me, as I stumble my way though life this way,
If I was a fly on the wall of my life, whatever would that fly say?

I'm not proud of what I am, but I strive to be much more,
To please me, to please God, and to please the fly watching me from atop the door,
I try to live for God, but I'm not perfect, and sometimes get a cross eye from the fly,
For he is privileged to see it all. . .every pitfall of my tired, trying life.

God hears each silent scream and sees every tear of mine that falls,
And there's only me and Him that know what goes on behind closed doors and walls.

If I was a fly on the wall, I'm sure it would all be clear,
If I was a fly on the wall, I whisper to myself not to fear,
If I was a fly on the wall, I would remind me that God's always near,
If I was a fly on the wall, I'd reassure myself God holds me dear.

Oh, the tales this fly could tell the world,
If he decided to spill every secret of mine,
Which he's witnessed me cry out to God,
On the bathroom floor, so many times,
Secrets so dark and buried deep,
That I wouldn't utter them to another living soul,

But I hide nothing from my Lord, my God. . .
I let Him in every nook and cranny and cavernous hole.

If I were a fly on the wall of my life,
What would I think? What would I advise?

I'd be watching myself wallow through this life without a spine,
Still bathing in my own sin, 'though Jesus tells me "Child, I'll take that as mine".
The fly would see my knees bend, breaking down before the Christ,
That's what the fly would see from the wall, if I happened to be that fly.

If I were a fly on the wall, I'd see
Exactly how much God does for me,
Not only does He set me free,
By breaking sin's chains so powerfully,
He loves, supports, and tends me daily,
He's faithful, graceful, and never fails me,
I don't get what I want, but I always see,
That The Lord provides everything I really need.

If I were a fly on the wall, I'd see
How I come before God so reverently,
On grateful, often trembling knees,
Knowing He'll handle me so lovingly.
He always deals with me compassionately,
When He draws near, I find it easy to breathe,
For this dark world tries to smother me,
And life's tests and trials bite constantly.

If I were a fly on the wall, I'd see
How much my own poor mind tortures me,
How anxiety's winds blow frantically,
And how dark and deep are depression's seas,
How the many regrets won't let me be,
How my Godless past is still haunting me,

How I feel like a no-one. . .unworthy. . .unclean,
Can't explain why The Shepherd decided to call me,
But I can't live without Him. . .this much I do see.

For God accepts my darkest spots,
And shines His light within their damaging shade,
Helping me to accept them too,
Or change the ones that are in need of change.

If I were a fly on the wall, peering into my own sin and soul,
Would I be okay with what I found? Would I accept my past and future road?
That's why the fly is there you see, to give you a bunch of extra eyes,
So even if a few of them are blinded by demons, you can still clearly see
The Christ.

"ARE YOU LIKE THE WILLOW OR THE OAK?"

Are you like the willow reaching for ground, with your branches stretching
out to sway,
Or like the oak that stands so mighty, firm in ground, dug in, rigid, set in
its ways?
Do your branches bend before The Lord, when pushed upon, as a willow
branch would bend,
Or do you stay quite rigid until you crack, as the oak wood's hardness does
intend?

Do your leaves bask in the sunlight, hanging down to recognize the Holy
clay,
Like the willow does trying to taste the goodness of Christ, grown from a
seed to praise?
Or like the oak, are you stern and hard, and remain inflexible in what you
see and believe,
Afraid to venture out of the shell and shelter the wooden planks provide
for thee?

Its solid wood seems stable to build from, and it provides a fine-looking,
sturdy frame,
But when all is said and done that's all that the oak offers, there's no soft-
ness to it in times of pain.
But when the willow drapes down on you, and wraps you in its soft, green,
warming grace,
It feels like the wings of Christ surrounding you, for the willow weeps in
Jesus's name.

The weeping willow bows its boughs, and gives its sad or happy tears gladly to Jesus Christ,
It sways in praise when buffeted by thunderstorms, and waves in praise when days are calm and bright.
The oak, 'though boughs reach upwards, it's all for show, and it doesn't really want to genuinely praise The Lord,
Unless He brings it only happy days, the oak goes limp and droops when fierce rain pours.

The oak is so set in its ways, and will not bend to God's wise timing, plan, and will,
So it creaks and groans when life's tempest comes, and keeps its old roots planted deep and still,
The willow trusts The Lord knows best, and allows Him to bend and shape its fragile frame,
Knowing that its branches will never break but can bounce back strong again in the power of Jesus's name.

The willow waits for The Lord to instruct it when to sprout or shed each pale green, luscious leaf,
It humbly displays its peaceful hues and shades to the glory of God in reverent faith and belief.
Whilst the oak presents its own splendor, expecting admiration from all when it shows off Autumn tones,
Or waits for the begging gratitude of creatures, as its brown acorns are scattered when ripe and grown.

When the sky begins to turn dark grey and Mother Nature's temper comes to play,
The willow's branches flex and sway, as the oak's branches still refuse to give way,
And as the wild wind whips and thunder roars, the raindrops soak the tree bark to core,
The willow embraces this and spreads out to soak up more, whilst the oak stands like a statue, and refuses to conform.

But the hard, unmoving oak finds itself in trouble, and breaks and uproots when trials bad weather arrives,
For it relies purely on its own strength and resilience and suffers deadly damage without the support of Christ.
The willow has faith that The Lord will provide it with shelter, strength, and stamina to survive harsh storms,
And if it lives, it lives in God's good grace, and if it's time, it will die and happily go be with The Lord.

Blessed is the weeping willow, for in life it knows it never weeps alone,
Its grateful foliage draping in the living water, as it bows before God's gracious throne,
But the oak's unmoved and brittle wood will make ideal kindling for The Devil's hellfire,
And the hard oak vainly digs its own grave and follows an arrogant trail towards its funeral pyre.

Are you the humble willow? Or are you the oak set in its ways?
Which way do your own leaves blow when the Devil's hand is raised?
Like the willow do you bow, and drape in obedience before the Christ?
Or are you more like the stubborn oak, set in your ways and still afraid of life?

"ONCE I WAS BLIND."

You love me with a love unrestrained,
You give to me in so many ways,
You fill the void when my mind strays,
But my human shell closes eyes to praise.

You give beyond great grace to me, love vibrant and alive,
'though it seems that all stays foggy when viewed through my human eyes.

I wish I could touch you Lord,
For then my human eyes could see
The grace that I am missing,
When my eyelids shut to Thee.

I wish that I could see. . .
Please Christ, grant that strength to me,
For I am your child, and to you I plea. . .

Oh please, my sweet Lord Christ,
Please open-up these blinded eyes.

Why can't I see what I need to see? . . .
Will I, once I have learned wise lessons from Thee?
When I've prayed enough on bended knee,
Or studied The Bible religiously?
When I've look inside my soul to see . . .
Just what it is that you ask of me?
Human eyes can LOOK, but they still refuse to SEE,
What it is that I need to be set free. . .
What I need to embrace you spiritually.

That's why I'm asking you today,
Lord, please take these dark scales away.

I long to see the path ahead,
I need to see your glorious face,
It's foggy, Lord, inside my head,
But still I'll walk with you by faith.

It's alright if my human eyes,
Can't see past this world's mortal ways,
For my soul can see quite perfectly,
And trusts you for eternal days.

I see all that I need to see –
I see enough, my Lord, to follow Thee,
Step forward, blind, if you need me to be,
For I love and trust you implicitly.

My faith requires no human eyes,
For I feel The Spirit's power inside,
And hope, light, love, and strength still rise,
Behind these clouded, weak, flesh, sightless eyes.

And then suddenly these eyes of mine are granted Holy sight,
Still blind to the darkness, but open to the bright of The Son of all light,
Colors, hues, becoming vibrant, as my mortal sight eagerly tastes the
Divine life,
Every image I'm allowed to behold is a gift to me granted by The Christ.

For so long I could not see a thing,
Until The Holy Spirit entered me,
Whilst I sat there blind on my bent knee,
With the touch of God washing over me,
Feeling stronger as He granted me strength and grace to see,
The chance at a Holy life. . .

A chance at the Holy dream. . .
All this through the gracious love He offers me.

Now my faith will stay strong and never fail,
My love for God will top any mortal scale.
In time, I trust you will descale. . .
When you're ready, I trust you will unveil,
To these yearning eyes, your righteous trail.

Until such time I'm pleased to be
A saved, redeemed child, Lord, of Thee,
Who promises to serve you faithfully,
And I can only view you from my knees.
I'm amazed you saved a wretch like me,
Flawed and undeserving, I hope you see the gratitude in me?
I know I'm nothing, Lord, without Thee,
And you have my heart and soul freely and reverently.
There's nothing more I need to see,
In this dark world. . .I'll leave it be,
For to walk with The Lord, oh glory be,
Is all I'll ever need to see.
Vision becoming sparkling. . .
Colors, vibrant, all new to me,
It seems that even the "blind" can see,
When you view not what your human eyes see,
Rather. . .a soul so wishing to be clean.

"SPIDERS AND WEBS."

Life seems so full of spider's webs,
With tangled weaves and sticky threads,
That pull, ensnare, entrap, and bind,
To stop our freedoms and twist our minds.

Is your web anorexia, anxiety, or grief?
Depression, cancer, pain, or lack of self-belief?
Is the spider The Devil, sin, or self as well?
Wrapped in stress, we can struggle, in these webs of hell.

So, who's the spider that eyes up you?
Eight beady pupils with dark, cold hues,
With an appetite for your pitied moans,
Your weak mind, heart, and flesh and bones.

Your enemy is always the spider,
Who wants to lure you in beside her,
So she can swallow you down inside her.

We are but weak, helpless flies drawn in to sticky webs,
Trapped, then, by the gossamer around our legs and heads,
Lies spun by the spiders can often keep us ensnared,
And we're unable to use our wings to flee into the air.

The spiders spin sinister silk to bind any unwitting soul,
Cocoon their victims, taunt them, nowhere for the prey to go,
Front legs make quick work spinning you, as the blanket neatly grows,
Silk strands starting to smother, trapping rancid sorrow in your soul.

Now caught and kept a prisoner, by this wicked, arachnid guard,
She keeps your soul fresh for The Devil, exposing the weakness in your heart,
She digs until she strikes the geyser of depression's oil, and opens up the pain,
Unable to move in your silk tomb, all you can do is desperately try to pray.

Every emotion that you know, causes the spider venom to break out,
Every sin ever born within you, every lie you've told, each time you tasted doubt,
Your knees won't bend, your hands are apart, but that's due to your spider cage,
You still control your heart and soul, so it's from these sanctuaries that you begin to pray. . .

"Dear Heavenly Father,
Please hear these words I pray,
And release me from this web today,
Circumstances have me trapped, my Lord,
The spider circles, my blood does roar,
Due to the venom pumping through
My weak veins and their sorrowed view.
Please give me strength to break these threads,
And truth to erase these feelings of dread,
Help me look this spider in the eye,
Defiantly, from where I lie,
Let it know I'm not a helpless victim,
For in any trials, you'll help me win.
Depression and grief cannot beat me,
Anorexia and anxiety won't defeat me,
For I am comforted by you Lord,
And I have my armor, shield, and sword.
I ask you, Father, please help me today,
Remove web's threads, in Jesus's name.
Amen".

In response, I feel a surge inside—and The Holy Spirit's fire consumes
The spider venom in my veins, replacing it with peace-filled hues,

The spider draws back just a little, and starts to look shocked and alarmed,
When she sees The Lord has given me strength to lift my head and move
my arms.

Determination in faith-filled eyes,
I use my sword to cut threads down to size,
She can't touch deep, for I have my shield,
I'm a child of God, so I shall not yield.
The spider's dazzled by the reflection of
The righteous breastplate and God's unfailing love,
And 'though the web is still sticky and dark,
It will never devour my soul's light spark,
For the source of this is The Christ Himself. . .
Light of the world, victor over death and Hell.

Soon the spider is tasting doom, as The Holy Spirit rises in me and shines,
The light shattering the spider's flesh, and dissolving all the silken twines,
And the darkest emotions and cruel fears, that once webbed over my mind,
Are taken freely from me, by my Savior Jesus Christ.

The cold air of the spider's lair now warming, dim gloom brightening to
light,
No longer shackled, no longer caged, no longer struggling withthe sins of life,
The Devil watches from his chamber, once again He has lost a soul to Christ,
But beware, for The Devil never gives up and recruits many spidery min-
ions to fight his fight.

There are many webs and many spiders,
For us to encounter on this road called life,
But keep the faith and you will find
They cannot steal your soul or light,
For we are more than conquerors,
Through Christ Jesus who loves us so much,
And God will always fight for us,
And liberate us from any harmful touch.

"WANDERING AND WONDERING."

Lately, I feel that my soul has been wondering,
It's been looking for something, and seeking, and pondering,
It senses there must be more to life than the flesh,
Something else than this world's choking, dark, broken mess,
And it wants to see a beacon as it calls S.O.S.

Lately, I feel that my soul has been wandering,
It's been looking for something, and seeking, and pondering,
It's restless, and breathless, and feels like it's dying,
It thirsts like a nomad who the desert sun's frying,
And shrivels like fallen leaf, all brown and drying.

Wondering,
Wandering,
Aimlessly around,
In my head,
On my feet,
In my heart,
In the clouds,
Wondering. . .lost,
And wandering. . .lost,
Not knowing how to solve this,
And what could be the cost.

I'm wondering what's caused this—
This unsettled feeling in my soul,
That makes such panic flood my veins,
And makes my human blood run cold.
I'm wandering, not knowing,

But searching for a way, a light, a sign,
Which will lead me to a happy place,
That will calm and restore my soul in time.

It seems I need a teacher, someone intelligent, confident, and wise,
To untangle these wandering, twisted twines, tying up my mind,
A fountain from which to drink of wisdom,
A respected mentor that my soul can learn from,
With love, like a loving Father, imparting wisdom about The Son.

It seems I need a Shepherd, a beacon to show my soul the way,
A guide to hold my hand tight, keeping soul from wandering astray,
A bright light beaming down to show the narrow way,
A compass to stir my soul North, towards Heaven's pearly gates,
A Father to lead His child to all the wonders that await.

Wondering,
And wandering,
Needing guidance and clarity. . .
Clarity in faith,
Guidance in fear,
Guidance for blind eyes,
Clarity to see through lies.
Wondering. . .seeking,
And wandering. . .seeking,
Not knowing where the answers lie,
But something inside me cries out "Christ!"

Once a wandering soul, now stops dead in its tracks,
For it's had an epiphany moment,
Blinded by The Light, like Saul on Damacus's road,
My wandering paths are straight now, instead of bent.
I see the cross so clearly now,
I hear The Shepherd's one, true voice,
My twisted mind stops wondering,
As Christ reveals Himself within soul's void.

No more wandering soul so lost and ailing,
No more wondering mind so panicked and flailing,
I have the answer to all I seek,
I'm ready to knock. . .I long to be one of His sheep.

The Truth, The Way, and The Life is clear,
I shall let no lies enter these mortal ears,
God pulls me close. . .I feel Him near,
My heart and soul overflow with joy and cheer.
He's the living water and I am a panting deer,
He's the bread of life who feeds me and takes away fear,
The Devil is nervous and starts to jeer,
But I'm drawn to The Gate with its grace-sign so clear.

Accepted, not rejected,
In Christ's grace and blood,
Salvation, rebirth,
The Holy's Spirit's great flood,
I'm allowed through The Gate that leads to the narrow way,
For I'm clean and redeemed, by Lord Jesus today.

And He'll stop me from wandering off of this path,
That's leads up to Heaven and peace-filled light-shafts,
And He'll stop me from wondering when the Earth and The Devil
Try to play with my mind, warp the view, trick, and meddle.

Wondering still. . . Although now with my thoughts crystal-clear,
Finding the answers I've been searching for, that let love conquer fear,
Restful in mind now, given the wisdom of Divine light,
Wondering still, but wondering now, how to better love and serve The Christ.

Wandering still. . . 'though now my blind eyes are allowed to see
The Holy, Righteous, narrow path The Shepherd has graciously granted me,
Two feet forever forward, down the narrow way to Heaven's clouds above,
Wandering still, but now wandering straight, under the wings of Jesus's
guiding love.

"FISHERMEN."

My Faith is the vessel that carries me,
And this mortal world is my raging sea,
I heard Him calling. . .I felt the need. . .
To serve my Christ from bended knees.

The Shepherd's voice rang loud and clear,
Whilst His grace allowed me to draw near,
Now His name's the sweetest thing to me,
And His truth and victory are all I see.

For I need this anchor in troubled seas,
To stop life's tempest from taking me
Down into dark and murky depths,
Full of hopeless currents, fears, and regrets.

I cling to God as my buoy and rock,
View Him as safe harbor in woes and shocks,
I want other people to have this strength too,
And experience His care in tides of deep blue.

Scripture explains to us the finest way to praise,
Is to do God's "good work" in Jesus's glorious name,
So I searched my soul for talents I could offer to my King,
And discovered a need to spread His Gospel growing grand inside of me.

So I board my boat, I built by belief and my blind faith,
And set sail to sea of souls, atop this world's white-water waves,
To my sorrow, I keep spying frightened souls and thriving sin,
Now I see, it is destiny for my soul to be, for Christ, a "Fisher of Men".

So I bait my hooks with words of Holy praise,
And cast my lines out to the rolling waves,
Praying that just a single, needy soul bites,
That I can reel in and introduce to the Christ.

Stray souls however are hard to harvest, as The Devil poisons
them with lies,
They become timid and complacent, blind to the brilliant light of
Christ.
So, I chum the water with Scripture, and drop anchor in the stills,
Sinking the nets, casting the rods, fishing for souls, all to God's will.

But this fisherman is human, and The Devil knows me well,
Often calling upon all of nature's wind and rage to cause the sea
to swell.
And my tiny craft, built by faith, is thrown about the waves,
As the hurricane circles above me I drop down to my knees and
pray.

I'm reminded of the story in The Bible where Jesus calms the
storm,
So I know that He is capable, and I'm certain He'll save me from
mortal harm,
But I don't know if He's willing to make the way ahead quite calm
and smooth,
For there're lessons to learn by weathering storms, and faith
grows strong in inclement hues.

So I simply cling on to my faith, my boat, as I am tossed around,
In trouble's seas, and Kraken's arms, and eddied far from solid
ground,
I realize this is where I'm supposed to be. . .in a place with others
floundering just like me,
So I can cast my fishing net and witness that The Lord still exists
far out at sea.

For where life's ocean is at its deepest, its deadliest, scariest, and its starkest,
Is where we all need God the most, and His Holy light shines brightest in
the darkness,
So while I'm trusting Him in storms, I can show my faith to others too,
And by drawing in any drowning souls, I hope they too will share faith's view.

I point towards His lighthouse, on The Rock, telling others not to fear,
For when we look past current strife, we can clearly see The Lord is near,
Although killer whales may circle round, and eyes are stung by these vast,
salty waves,
We can rely upon our Holy Father, His unfailing grace, and the power of
Jesus's name.

So, each day I pack my tackle, brave the storm, with bait-box snapped,
Fishing for souls that have lost their way, feeling forgotten, lost, and trapped,
And once aboard my boat, I shall shuttle them to the lighthouse on Jesus's
shores,
So that they may taste the grace that spawned my faith and receive love
from Christ forevermore.

Humbled, proud, honored, and blessed, that The Lord saw fit to call me to
this task,
This faithful, loyal, and loving fisherman, will do whatever God may ask,
For I'm glad to know and love The Lord, and want others to have this pas-
sion too,
So I will throw my nets out daily, to show the world the way to Salvation's
bright view.

"BEQUEATH."

I'm not rich in worldly terms,
So I don't have much to bequeath,
When death finally comes a-knocking,
And this human life I finally leave,
But I hope my lasting legacy
Will be one of hope and love and faith and light,
And I'm remembered for spreading the message
Of soul's Salvation through The Lord God Jesus Christ.

I have witnessed the same world that you have seen,
I have been touched by sorrow, tasted joy, and everything in between,
I have lived through life's trials, so many life lessons have been learned,
To qualify me for Heaven and shield me from the Hellfire's burn.

So what is it I bequeath? What stamp do I leave on this mortal land?
For I lived my life to honor Christ, holding tight onto His hand,
I tried to spread love as He spreads love, tried to support like Him my fel-
low Man,
Preached His word and message to the world the best this simple servant
can.

I hope I have bequeathed
The strength of faith God gives to me,
I hope that people see,
The battles I have won because of He,
He who bequeaths us everything,
Forgiveness, Salvation, and the promise of
A life of bliss in Glory,
In the presence of our loving God.

I hope that others see God's grace,
Etched on my fragile, thankful face,
To show that I can only stand
Each day because He holds my hand.
Do I bequeath a sample of
God's support, His power, strength, and love?
By showing my dependence upon
His tending hand and wings that shelter from above.

Do I bequeath my reverence?
Do I bequeath my steadfast trust in God?
Do I bequeath the fruits He's grown in me?
Do I bequeath examples of His love?

Do I bequeath my prayers and heartfelt praise?
Do I bequeath how God has rescued me,
More times than I can mention,
When I'm tossed and torn in troubled seas.

Do I bequeath my pilgrim's path?
Have I shown to others the route to His narrow way?
Have I bequeathed the stark truth's warning,
About when Jesus Christ comes back one day?

I hope I have bequeathed my weakness,
I hope that I have shown my flaws,
I hope that people know
That I am nothing without The Almighty Lord.
I hope to bequeath my sanctification,
I hope to show my satisfaction,
With the blessings God has given me,
Even when I struggle and cannot see.

So, as I transcend to meet my God, off to my eternity,
Reflecting on a life, I am only now appreciating,

I bequeath my thankful love to kith and kin, as I let this world go,
And with the arms of my heart wide open, I bequeath to Christ my eternal soul!

"OLD."

(A poetic short story written
by Suzanne Newman & Michael Grgich—MAG)

On a small hill, not so far away, there hangs an old and worn-out swing,
Made from a plank of old shed-wood, tied to a tree with thick, frayed string,
It rocks, abandoned, on this hill, is weathered, aged, with jagged sides,
Far cry from its young glory days, when it used to give the kids great rides.
The wooden seat is cracked and old and flaking due to years of rain,
This swing would love to swing so high again but could not take the strain.

Likewise, there's an old lady, who been dreaming of her past-youth's days,
Reminisces 'bout the swing she misses, and wonders if it still does sway.
She moves her tired, old, shaking bones and takes her walking stick in hand,
And shuffles down the road until the houses fade and she sees land.
The lady looks across the field, to the old farm where she did grow up,
She used to play within this meadow, make daisy chains, pick buttercups,
And in the distance, if she looks, stares hard and squints with aging eyes,
She thinks she spies her old swing, on the hill, which is a nice surprise!

It takes a while for her to walk across the field to reach the hill,
For old legs don't move very fast, and old heart is feeling rather ill,
She stops to catch her breath a minute, before attempting, then, to scale
The small hill there before her, but she perseveres, although she's frail.
She smiles a huge nostalgic smile, when finally the peak she sees,
And spots her homemade childhood swing, still hanging from the cherry
tree.
The lady's old and gnarly hands reach out and touch the fraying string,
Then, lovingly, she caresses the rotting wood upon her favorite swing.
She wonders if she sits on it again if it will take her weight?

For many years have passed and many pounds put on since she was eight!
So, gingerly and gently, this old lady lowers her bottom down
Upon the wooden plank-seat, which surprisingly still holds its ground.
She won't attempt to swing it, but sits happily rocking to and fro,
Thinking about the decades past, perplexed at where the time did go.

Her mind sways to reflection, for she sees her end-time drawing near,
And when, inside our souls we relive past life, we recall every year.

A push, a cry, a struggle. . .this old woman as a baby born,
Looking with love into the eyes of those who brought her into this world.
At that first moment it was wondrous, a gift of love and ecstasy,
But that is not how life turned out, as she relives, let's watch and see. . .

The old woman kicks with all she has, but still she barely moves the swing,
Looking deep into the clouds, she starts once again remembering. . .
A baby in a high-chair, being babysat by the big T.V.,
Alone in her little infant world, as parents are seldom seen.
But, then, it's grand! Off to toddler land, friends to replace her missing home,
Mom and dad don't have time? She screams to Heaven, "I'll do it Alone!"
Down the hill in a cardboard box, to the tree house all her friends had built,
Spending time with friends instead of family, 'though her young heart filled
with a touch of guilt.
Toddler into adolescent, a young lass is grown and curious,
'though her clan itself is not Godly, this girl wants, she needs, she quests,
To find something beyond the now, something her faith could shelter in,
A shelter for her love, her soul, so her Spiritual journey is about to begin.

As her teenage-self raises its ugly head, denying dark, she ran to God instead,
No hate grew in her mortal heart, she wished with righteousness to wed,
She snuck off to church one foggy morn, so stealthily,—parents unaware,
And she basked, so thankful, within the word of God and the wonderous
truth found there.
As she sat there, singing gospel, a young stallion caught her gleaming eye,
It seemed to be a message, as if this love was sent from Jesus Christ.
Eye to eye and heart to heart, two strangers, loving, soul to soul,

As this old woman keeps trying to sway the swing. . . where now will her memories go?

An old woman still trying desperately to swing,
In her own mind swoons on a treasured memory,
Of the man in church she could not unsee,
a soulmate she felt from the first smile's beam.
He approached, shy and subdued
And said "ma'am if you could give me the honor,
I'd love to court you for a night and prove I am what you're after".
Her eyes batted to reflect the sky, her excited smile shows no calm,
As she takes this boy within her arms and tells him "I'm yours, forever long"!
Two souls soon become one and live in close unity,
But there is much more here to come from the old woman sat upon the swing.

Marrying her childhood sweetheart, both were thrilled that they had met at church,
This woman thanked The Good Lord, that their love did heal the years of hurt—
Hurt by neglective parents, but now as a bride, she could move out
Form her old home, where she grew up, which she was very glad about.

Years of happiness went by, two babies born. . .so sweet their cries!
A boy, a girl, both born from love, and both were apples of her eyes.
She thanked The Lord for family, for husband and kids of her own,
For food upon their table, for such love and for a happy home.

Until that day, when it was ripped away. . .

A tear rolls down the cheek of the old lady as she rocks the swing,
Reliving bad, old memories. . .heart re-breaking as the sorrow swims,
For she remembers all too well, the day there came a knock upon
Her front door. . .it was the police. . . "ma'am, I'm sorry, it's about your husband and son. . ."

"There's been a car crash," he went on, "I'm sorry, ma'am, but they're both dead".
The woman rushed upstairs, to where her daughter lay asleep in bed.
"She's only five, how can I tell her daddy and brother are both gone?"
She fell down on her grieving knees. . .cried for her true love and young son.
Lifting her eyes to Heaven, she screamed: "Why Lord? I don't understand!"
Heart hardening in anger, she replaced prayers with stiff, fisted hands.

The once well-thumbed big Bible, then sits unused, dusty, on the shelf,
The woman too distressed, caught up in hatred, loss and grief's dark hell.
Times were tough financially, but her daughter and her still stayed close,
Despite the times of hunger, repaired shoes, used books and thrift-store clothes.
She tried to count her blessings, but the woman found life too unfair,
And refused to listen to God's voice. . .refused to believe He was there.

An old woman stands up and leaves the swing,
Torn by the visions her old mind brings,
But looking back to that frail, shed-wood,
She understands this healing is good,
These memories are stinging,
But closure they're bringing.

Years spent tending closely, as her fragile, lonely daughter grows,
Trying to be the best she can be, to give her daughter, a mother, a home,
But the child soon strays and lashes out, and then mom becomes the enemy,
Wild, violent, and troubled, 'til confused tears then grace her mother's cheek.
One day at dinner, just the two of them, her daughter cruelly lashes out,
"Why did they have to die mom? Was it your fault?" through her tears she shouts.

The old woman's eyes just well-up, as she relives this hurtful memory,
As she sits, kicking her feet, on the wooden swing, swaying in the summer breeze.

Years passed and her young daughter heals, but the woman remains a little unsure,
For she's wrestled grief for many years and it has left the both of them so sore,
But hopefully she accepts it, and then later her girl claims a beau,
She accepts him into her heart, with her daughter, and welcomes him into her humble home.

Time ticks along as time will bring,
Back in the here and now and the old woman still swings.
Now moving to and fro. . . pushing hurt old hips, kicking up sore knees,
This old woman still visualizes her past dreams,
Now lost deep within her memories.

She continues to rock on the swing. . .

As a younger woman, fallen from faith, far from God with a hate not known before,
This lady was cooking the dinner, when then comes a loud rap upon her own front door. . .
Dressed in a uniform, the firefighter relayed to her,
"There was a massive fire ma'am. . .at the farm. We believe your parents both perished and burned."

She fell, wallowing, to the floor, in tears, her soul re-broken and re-torn,
She screams aloud in agony, "Can this cruel world hurt me any more?"
"Dear God, please stir me back home,
I know I've strayed so far from your throne,
I'm sorry, but now I need some strength,
For I'm floundering and sorrow's too long in length."

The old woman is so tired now, but rocks in the wind upon the swing,
But still reaching for more answers, she embraces these pained memories.
She hangs her head before The Lord, ashamed when she recalls that time,
When she was lost in bitterness and strayed from Him in heart and mind,
But, thankfully, her soul fought-on, would not give in and made her pray,
And in her deep distress, she cried out "Father" on that fateful day. . .

So, in her suffering and heartbreak, this young woman stayed down on her knees,
Struggling, all alone inside, to come to terms with all her grief,
When suddenly, she hears a gentle voice above her sobbing tears,
It was The Lord, who came to comfort her and tell her He is near!
The woman's heart was shocked, yet hopeful, glad that she could feel God's love,
Soul's eyes began descaling, in revelations from The Lord above.
She realized that turning from Him in harsh times just made her pain much worse,
For Jesus understands, and His love and compassion lessen hurt.
The woman's stunned and shaking, for she thought that God abandoned her,
Knows now that SHE abandoned HIM, and a thousand thoughts and feelings whir.

She quickly rises to her feet and races to the bookcase shelf,
In search of her old Bible, now her heart has warmed, she thaws and melts.
She blows the dust off, (quite embarrassed), and wipes the faded, leather cover,
Tries to calm herself, as she is eager for its wisdom to discover.
Every page The Lord does draw her to turns out to explain much,
And with each verse, her pain decreases. . .lessens with God's loving touch.

The woman sees the error of her ignorant and faithless days,
Wants to go forwards with The Lord and calls on His amazing grace.
She finds herself back on her knees. As Jesus Christ accepts her pleas,
The Holy Spirit fills her up, with cleansing fire and gives her peace.

Now smiling as she sways the swing, the old woman looks up to the sky,
Thanking God for being there, and for her Salvation through Jesus Christ.
For this has brought her comfort. . .given hope. . .perspective, over the years,
And trusting in His will and guidance has saved her many woeful tears.
She realizes through all her pain, God didn't leave her in distress,
And although life's been difficult, she still sees how He left her blessed.

Her daughter now has daughters of her own and has a happy home,
Lives nearby so her mother doesn't feel abandoned or alone.
And from her hilltop viewpoint, The old lady spies, not far away,
That house and 4 granddaughters in the garden, as they run and play.
"I wonder what their future brings?" she thinks as she daydreams on the swing.

She pauses for a moment. . .her reflective mood now worn and meek,
Tears streaming from her wrinkly eyes, her hand wipes off her weary cheeks,
She remembers all the grandkids born. . . the date and time of every one,
She remembers how they smelt and felt, when she got to hold each precious one.
It doesn't seem that long ago, when she herself was just a girl,
Innocent and just playing, oblivious to the ways of this cruel world,
But adulthood can be so harsh, caught in a whirl of grief and stress,
And now the woman's old and tired, and body is far from its best.

She leans her head against the string, which smells damp as it's old and fraying,
Creaking noises come from the swing's wooden seat, for it's decaying,
"My old friend", she speaks to the swing, "I understand. . .for I rot too,
My heart is fading quickly, and this cancer riddles me all through".
The old woman's mind now wallows, thinking back to what the doctor said,
"Ummm. . . ma'am I'm truly sorry, but within 3 months you will be dead.
I know this is a shock ma'am, and I hope you'll take this news okay?
Please know my thoughts are with you" she heard the doctor sigh and say.

But she's a woman with strong conviction and far from Satan's easy prey,
She will still kneel down to her God, 'though her legs ache, she still bends to pray.
Her faith keeps driving forward, for she knows reverse will mean she falls,
She lapsed once, will not lapse again! For she trusts The Christ's great victory call.
She pauses for a moment. . .halts the sway of her old rickety swing,
For 'though her hearing's aging, her ears prick up as the angels sing. . .

Despite all the old memories, this old lady dredges through her mind,
Old wounds, old love, old grief, old pain, she still believes The Lord is kind,
And now a gentle, peaceful feeling, washes her like warming tides,
A calm and happy presence of God's love does fill her up inside. . .

"Hello, my child", says Christ's voice, as He stands beside her at the swing,
"I've come to take you home now and remember death has lost its sting.
I've made a room for you, my daughter, saved a seat at the wedding table,
I forgive all your past sins, and you've shown me that your faith is strong
and stable.
Come now, child, and don't look back, for you won't need this old human
shell,
I'll clothe you, fit for Heaven, where my sweet flock all do rest and dwell".

The old woman stands up gladly. . .steps up with Christ. . .won't pause to
look back,
For if she did, she'd see the swing was broken now and string had snapped.
Her mortal body laying slumped upon the grass, atop that hill,
Her ailing heart stopped beating. . .lungs stopped breathing. . .pulse has
gone quite still.
But onwards goes her spirit. . .onwards. . .upwards to her Heaven's home,
Happy, hand in hand with Christ, to where all other saints have flown.
The woman's sad and weary tears, now turn to tears of bliss and joy,
As she kisses this sad world goodbye, there's no more woe to hurt or toy.
She smiles and looks to Jesus. . .thanks Him for His grace and love so pure,
His understanding and compassion, for Salvation that reassures.
As gently they stroll through the clouds, each step she's nearer Heaven's gates,
The woman feels much younger, starts to heal, and grief no longer grates.
And when they reach the entrance to God's kingdom, the gates open wide,
For Heaven's been expecting her. . .and with Jesus, she walks on inside.

A WORD OF THANKS

I just want to thank my dear friend and brother in Christ Jesus
Michael Grgich for giving me permission to share just some of
our collaborations in this book.

Michael and I have been writing collabs together since 2020. I
live in England while Michael lives in California, U.S.A. We met
through Christian poetry on Facebook and our kinship and writ-
ing partnership has grown from there.
(Michael usually signs his poetry with the tag MAG)

I also want to thank YOU. . .the reader, for buying (or borrowing)
this book and taking the time to read the poems, I really hope
you enjoyed it and received the message that God IS with us in
every difficulty and circumstance imaginable in life. So, please be
reassured in your faith my Christian kin, knowing you never fight
battles alone, and that you are treasured and protected by The
Great "I AM".

May God bless you all.

All glory to God for ever and ever.

SECTION THREE

PERSONAL TESTIMONY OF SUZANNE NEWMAN.

To be honest, I'm not sure where to start with this! Do I include my life's history, details of childhood etc.? I do have to be aware of family members who will read this and don't really feel the need to let the entire world know every single thing about me. So, all that being said, I plan to keep this fairly brief!

I was brought up in a household where God wasn't really talked about, although we did celebrate Christmas. The Lord's name was regularly used as a swear-word and on the rare occasion prayer was mentioned, I was given the impression that it was to ask for something—a bit like a Christmas list for Santa! My Grandad was an atheist most of his life, but my Nan was a believer and went to chapel every Sunday. She was a private lady and never really discussed her faith with me. I didn't go to school with anyone who had a strong religious conviction and didn't know any neighbors that went to church/synagogue/mosque etc. Due to all this, serious thoughts of God never really entered my head until I was in my late-teens, but looking back I always felt He was there—I never thought He DIDN'T exist, I just didn't think much about His existence, or what His role was and what He meant to my life personally.

When I was 18 years old, I suddenly felt like there was a huge hole inside of me. I didn't know what it could be, but quickly worked-out that it was a Spiritual need of some sort. I spent the next 18 months speaking to work colleagues and anyone else I could about their religious beliefs, in order to find the "right" religion for me to commit to. But, to my confusion and panic, I soon discovered that none of them felt right!

Then, a new lady started work at our place and she explained to me that she was a "born-again Christian". She told me what that

149

meant and precisely what she believed in. Everything suddenly clicked into place inside of me and I knew without a single doubt that this was what I had been searching for, or rather, what God had been calling me to and I just hadn't realized! To me, this wasn't a "religion" as such, but rather a way of life, led by a belief in the Triune God and being saved through trust and faith in The Lord Jesus Christ as Messiah.

This lady and her husband spent many evenings talking with me about their beliefs, answering my questions etc. Then one evening, a group of us had gone out for a meal and it ended up with me back at her house at 3a.m., kneeling on the floor in tears of repentance and happiness as I professed my faith in Jesus Christ in prayer and asked Him to come into my life. I didn't think He would, because why would he want ME? But to my amazement, relief and sheer joy He graciously accepted my contrite heart and sent The Holy Spirit to wash over me like a warm flood from top to toe!

I left my friend's house at 6a.m. a grateful and changed person— clean, re-born, renewed, indestructible, no longer part of or afraid of this mortal world, and filled with the joy that can only come from knowing you are saved by The Lord. I wanted to shout it from the roof tops and tell the world how great God is. . . . .and I still do, over 30yrs later!

Thank you Jesus!

Well, that's how I came to God all those years ago, but a lot has happened since then! I have cared for loved-ones with Senile Dementia, had two children, suffered an ectopic pregnancy, had surgery to remove tumors, survived (against all medical odds) a rare and very aggressive cancer in 2015/16, came back from the brink of suicide and wage an ongoing battle with clinical anxiety and depression to this day. But I have witnessed first-hand during all these testing times how The Lord is with us throughout and gives us strength, stamina and wisdom when we have none left of our own. God is our comfort and light in the darkest of times. . .without fail.

The Lord prompted me to write poetry about my times of struggle two years after my cancer journey. I have found this not only cathartic for me personally, but by sharing these poems via publishing books and posting on Facebook, I can try (in some small way) to humbly encourage others who are going through similar testing times, by witnessing to God's greatness and showing how He has been there for me. I have had much positive feedback from people in this sense so far—all glory to God for that. I acknowledge I am nothing without Him and thank Him every day for all He does, not only for me, but for everyone who has been saved in The Lord Jesus Christ and have the blessed privilege to be called "children of light".

We serve a faithful and loving God indeed, who is worthy of all praise.

SECTION FOUR

BIBLE VERSES

Here are some encouraging Bible verses to end this book with, because I don't want you to take just my word for it that God is loving, awesome and never leaves us to struggle alone. These are just a few. . .there are so many more! Praise The Lord!
(All Scripture quotes are taken from the NIV translation).

Isaiah 41:13 –
"For I am the Lord your God who takes hold of your right hand and says to you, Do not fear, I will help you."

Deuteronomy 31:8 –
"The Lord Himself goes before you and will be with you; He will never leave you nor forsake you. Do not be afraid; Do not be discouraged."

Psalm 94:18&19 –
"When I said, "My foot is slipping," your unfailing love, Lord, supported me. When anxiety was great within me, your consolation brought me joy."

Matthew 11:28–30 –
"Come to me, all you who are weary and burdened, and I will give you rest. Take my yoke upon you, and learn from me, for I am gentle and humble in heart, and you will find rest for your souls. For my yoke is easy, and my burden is light."

John 14:27 –
"Peace I leave with you; my peace I give you. I do not give to you as the world gives. Do not let your hearts be troubled and do not be afraid."

Isaiah 41:10 –
"So do not fear, for I am with you; do not be dismayed, for I am your God; I will strengthen you and help you, I will uphold you with my righteous right hand."

Psalm 27:1 –
"The Lord is my light and my salvation—whom shall I fear? The Lord is the stronghold of my life—of whom shall I be afraid?"

Philippians 4:6&7 –
"Do not be anxious about anything, but in every situation, by prayer and petition, with thanksgiving, present your requests to God. And the peace of God, which transcends all understanding, will guard your hearts and your minds in Christ Jesus."

Romans 8:28 –
"And we know that in all things God works for the good of those who love Him, who have been called according to His purpose."

Joshua 1:9 –
"Have I not commanded you? Be strong and courageous. Do not be afraid; do not be discouraged, for the Lord your God will be with you wherever you go."

Proverbs 3:5&6 –
"Trust in the Lord with all your heart, and lean not on your own understanding; in all your ways submit to Him, and He will make your paths straight."

Isaiah 43:1&2-
"Do not fear, for I have redeemed you; I have summoned you by name; you are mine. When you pass through the waters, I will be with you; and when you pass through the rivers, they will not sweep over you. When you walk through the fire, you will not be burned; the flames will not set you ablaze."

2 Corinthians 4:16–18 –
"Therefore we do not lose heart. Though outwardly we are wasting away, yet inwardly we are being renewed day by day. For our light and momentary troubles are achieving for us an eternal glory that far outweighs them all. So we fix our eyes not on what is seen, but on what is unseen, since what is seen is temporary, but what is unseen is eternal."

1 Peter 5:7 –
"Cast all your anxiety on Him, because He cares for you".

James 1:2–4 –
"Consider it pure joy, my brothers and sisters, whenever you face trials of many kinds, because you know that the testing of your faith produces perseverance. Let perseverance finish its work so that you may be mature and complete, not lacking anything."

Hebrews 13:5–6 –
"Keep your lives free from the love of money and be content with what you have, because God has said, "Never will I leave you; never will I forsake you". So we say with confidence, "The Lord is my helper; I will not be afraid. What can mere mortals do to me?"

Romans 8:38–39 –
"For I am convinced that neither death nor life, neither angels nor demons, neither the present nor the future, nor any powers, neither height nor depth, nor anything else in all creation, will be able to separate us from the love of God that is in Christ Jesus our Lord."

Psalm 121:1&2 –
"I life up my eyes to the hills. From where does my help come? My help comes from the Lord, the Maker of heaven and earth."

Hebrews 6:19 –
"We have this hope as an anchor for the soul, firm and secure."

Psalm 16:8 –
"I keep my eyes always on the Lord. With Him at my right hand, I will not be shaken."

John 16:33 –
"I have told you these things, so that in me you may have peace. In this world you will have trouble. But take heart! I have overcome the world."

Psalm 46:1–3 –
"God is our refuge and strength, an ever-present help in trouble. Therefore, we will not fear, though the earth give way and the mountains fall into the heart of the sea, though its waters roar and foam and the mountains quake with their surging."

Isaiah 40:31 –
"But those who hope in the Lord will renew their strength. They will soar on wings like eagles; they will run and not grow weary; they shall walk and not be faint."

Psalm 73:26 –
"My flesh and my heart may fail, but God is the strength of my heart and my portion forever".

James 1:12 –
"Blessed is the one who perseveres under trial because, having stood the test, that person will receive the crown of life that the Lord has promised to those who love Him".

Matthew 19:26 –
"Jesus looked at them and said, "With man this is impossible, but with God all things are possible".

Hebrews 2:18 –
"Because He Himself suffered when He was tempted, He is able to help those who are being tempted".

Psalm 147:3 –
"He heals the broken-hearted and binds up their wounds".

Psalm 91:4 –
"He will cover you with His feathers, and under His wings you will find refuge".

Matthew 1:23 –
"The virgin will conceive and give birth to a son, and they will call Him Immanuel, (which means "God with us")".

FURTHER INFORMATION

For those of you who may be interested, I have an author page on Facebook.
The address is facebook.com/snewmanpoetry.

I currently have three other Christian poetry books on sale internationally on many online retailers including Amazon. The titles are:

"It's Not Just You!"
(written by Suzanne Newman.)

"Inspired By. . ."
(written by Suzanne Newman and Michael Grgich—MAG.)

"Kindred Spirits."
(written by Suzanne Newman and Michael Grgich   MAG,
and including cover artwork and bespoke images inside by
American artist Debra Whelan.)

ALL GLORY TO GOD. . .
ALWAYS.

www.ingramcontent.com/pod-product-compliance
Lightning Source LLC
Chambersburg PA
CBHW060312100426
42812CB00003B/762